Reformed and Catholic

Reformed and Catholic

Essays in Honor of Peter Toon

EDITED BY
Roberta Bayer

PICKWICK *Publications* · Eugene, Oregon

REFORMED AND CATHOLIC
Essays in Honor of Peter Toon

Copyright © 2012 Wipf and Stock. All rights reserved. Except for brief quotations in critical publications or reviews, no part of this book may be reproduced in any manner without prior written permission from the publisher. Write: Permissions, Wipf and Stock Publishers, 199 W. 8th Ave., Suite 3, Eugene, OR 97401.

Pickwick Publications
An Imprint of Wipf and Stock Publishers
199 W. 8th Ave., Suite 3
Eugene, OR 97401

www.wipfandstock.com

ISBN 13: 978–1-61097–688–6

Cataloging-in-Publication data:

Reformed and catholic : essays in honor of Peter Toon / edited by Roberta Bayer.

xxx + 114 p. ; 23 cm. Includes bibliographical references and index.

ISBN 13: 978–1-61097–688–6

1. Cranmer, Thomas, 1489–1556. 2. Anglican Communion—Liturgy—Texts—History. 3. Church of England, Book of common prayer—History. 4. Hooker, Richard, 1553 or 4–1600. I. Toon, Peter, 1939–2009. II. Bayer, Roberta. III. Title.

BX5145 B213 2012

Manufactured in the U.S.A.

To my husband and children

Contents

Contributors

Roberta L. Bayer is Assistant Professor of Government at Patrick Henry College, and holds a doctorate in Government from the University of Notre Dame, an M.A. in Medieval Studies from the University of Toronto, and an M.Sc.in Political Philosophy from the London School of Economics. Dr. Bayer edits the magazine of the Prayer Book Society of the United States, the *Anglican Way*. She has written on George Parkin Grant and specializes in medieval and contemporary political thought.

Roger T. Beckwith is a priest of the Church of England holding an Oxford BD and Lambeth DD. Formerly Warden of Latimer House, Oxford, his publications include *The Old Testament Canon of the New Testament Church*, and *Calendar and Chronology, Jewish and Christian*. Most recently he has written *Praying with Understanding: Explanations of Words and Passages in the Book of Common Prayer*.

Graham Eglington is an Australian born and Australian and English educated lawyer (retired), ordained in Canada. He was National Director of the Prayer Book Society of Canada, 1990–99, in which capacity he continued a close collaboration with the late Peter Toon that had begun in the 1980s through the Prayer Book Society in Ottawa of which Fr. Eglington was the founding Chairman. While in private practice in Ottawa he served as Counsel to the Standing Joint Committee of the Senate and House of Commons of Canada on Regulations and Other Statutory Instruments, and as Counsel to the Security and Intelligence Review Committee of the Queen's Privy Council for Canada. He was a member of the Immigration Appeal Board before becoming National Director of the Prayer Book Society of Canada.

Gillis J. Harp received his doctorate in American history from the University of Virginia in 1986 and has taught at McGill University and Acadia University in Nova Scotia, before coming to Grove City College in 1999 where he is a professor in the Department of History. His publications include *Positivist Republic: Auguste Comte and the Reconstruction of American Liberalism, 1965–1920* and *Brahmin Prophet: Phillip Brooks and the Path of Liberal Protestantism*. Gillis had been an active layman in Anglican circles since the mid-1980s; he and his wife and daughters worship at Grace Anglican Church (ACNA) in Slippery Rock, Pennsylvania.

The Rev Dr. Rudolph Heinze has a doctorate from the University of Iowa and an Honorary Doctor of Letters from Concordia University. He is a priest in the Church of England, and a Canon of the Diocese of Port Sudan. He has published three books and numerous scholarly articles. His most recent publication is a study of the sixteenth-century Reformation, entitled *Reform and Conflict: From the Medieval World to the Wars of Religion, 1350–1648*.

Joan Lockwood O'Donovan is a theologian and academic who has lectured and written extensively in Christian political and social thought. Her books include: *George Grant and the Twilight of Justice*, *Theology of Law and Authority in the English Reformation*, *From Irenaeus to Grotius: A Sourcebook in Christian Political Thought*, co-edited with Oliver O'Donovan, and *Bonds of Imperfection: Christian Politics Past and Present*, co-authored with Oliver O'Donovan. She has been a consultant editor and regular reviewer for *Studies in Christian Ethics*, and currently holds an honorary fellowship at New College, University of Edinburgh. She has published a number of articles on the history of the *Book of Common Prayer*.

Ian Robinson was a pupil of F. R. Leavis at Cambridge and lectured in English Language and Literature for many years in the University of Wales. He was co-founder of The Brynmill Press Ltd. Publications include *The Survival of English, Cranmer's Sentences* and *Who Killed the Bible?* Ian Robinson collaborated with Peter Toon in producing a number of books including *The Homilies Appointed to be Read in Churches*; the only modern edition.

Bryan D. Spinks is Goddard Professor of Liturgical Studies and Pastoral Theology, Yale Institute of Sacred Music and Yale Divinity School. His most recent books are *Early and Medieval Rituals and Theologies of Baptism: From the New Testament to the Council of Trent*; *Reformation and Modern Rituals and Theologies of Baptism: From Luther to Contemporary Practices*; *Liturgy in the Age of Reason: Worship and Sacraments in England and Scotland, 1662–c.1800*; and *The Worship Mall: Liturgical Initiatives and Responses in a Postmodern Global World*. Professor Spinks is coeditor of the *Scottish Journal of Theology*, a former consultant to the Church of England Liturgical Commission, president emeritus of the Church Service Society of the Church of Scotland, and a fellow of the Royal Historical Society and of Churchill College, Cambridge.

Introduction

ROBERTA BAYER

The Purpose of this Volume

The Reverend Dr. Peter Toon (1939–2009) was the best-known defender of Anglican orthodoxy and the Book of Common Prayer throughout the last decades of the twentieth century. He was a tutor of theology in colleges and seminaries, parish priest, and President of the Prayer Book Society of the United States during a very productive and energetic life. He wrote many books and pamphlets and numerous internet essays, so having a great influence on Anglicans around the world.

These essays have been written by his fellow scholars, and are of both scholarly and general interest. It is hoped that this collection will encourage a revival of interest in Dr. Toon's work and so also renewed respect for historical Anglican theology and Cranmer's Book of Common Prayer. The Book of Common Prayer is praiseworthy for the moderation and wisdom contained within its theology and rites, its capacity to produce reverence for God, and to excite piety among believers. Anglicanism, in its origins, combined evangelism with a catholic and reverent liturgy. Its liturgy, as compiled by Cranmer contains the true gospel; it is the Bible set to prayer. Yet in the beauty of its liturgy, the symbolic power of the sacraments, the depth of its spirituality, and its episcopate, it is heir to the universal church.

Anglicanism holds to the central teachings of the faith; it contains within its doctrines everything which must be known for salvation. In *The Anglican Way* (1983) Peter Toon stated:

> what I shall do in this book is to present a definite picture of An-
> glicanism as called by God, in these days when there is much talk
> of Church unity, to set an example for the world-wide Church
> in terms of her simultaneous commitment to the Evangel and to
> Catholicity. I do not, in any way, want to unchurch members of
> other denominations and groups, but I do want to call Episcopa-
> lians (Anglicans) to the full realization of what their God-given
> position in Christendom should mean today. Without appearing
> to be arrogant, I would want to say that, just as ancient Israel was
> set by God to be a light to the nations, so I see the Anglican Com-
> munion of Churches set by God, in the midst of all the Churches,
> to be a light—providing a luminous example of simultaneous
> commitment to the Gospel and to Catholicity.[1]

This is a strong statement, and quite remarkable in its way. He said that the
Anglican Church is not called to be evangelical in its preaching and catholic in its liturgy, nor is it called to be sometimes evangelical and sometimes
catholic, rather the history of the Anglican Church shows that it is called
to be simultaneously wholly evangelical and wholly catholic.[2] Few people
within the Anglican family of churches can comprehend this because aban-
donment of the Anglican way has led to disunity. It is my hope that the
essays in this volume will help to reveal to readers the unity and truth of
that original theological vision, the catholic and evangelical character of the
theology of Anglicanism, and its continuing importance.

A Brief Summary of the Essays

Joan Lockwood O'Donovan's article "Worship, the Moral Life, and Community: The Cranmerian Prayer Book Legacy" addresses the political theology
of Thomas Cranmer, Archbishop of Canterbury, martyr, and architect of
the Anglican settlement during Edward VI's reign. Dr. O'Donovan argues
that Cranmer envisioned for England a Christian church and a Christian
state with a public liturgy at its ceremonial center. Ceremonies are for the
good of man, as Cranmer wrote in his *Of Ceremonies* (1549), because ceremonies properly constructed are "apt to stir up the dull mind of man to
the remembrance of his duty to God." If Protestant England was to be a
truly Christian society, a model for Christendom, composed of people of all

---

1. Toon, *Anglican Way*, 15.
2. Ibid., 13.

ranks, all obedient in the faith, it required a public liturgy to renew moral agency and action. Although rulers in a commonwealth with an established church are in danger of confusing temporal and spiritual powers, Cranmer hoped that true religion expounded in the churches would allow them to distinguish spiritual offices and temporal powers, so that justice would result in church and commonwealth by the grace of God. Bishops were to teach, their chief duty was to proclaim the gospel.

When Queen Mary ascended the throne of England, she returned the Church of England to Roman Catholicism and Cranmer found himself in a difficult position as Archbishop. Given Cranmer's political theology, he knew that he must submit to his sovereign in matters of public law. Consequently he had to choose between his conviction that as Archbishop he must honor the Queen who has legal jurisdiction in the realm, and his obligation to proclaim the gospel. This complex situation led to his martyrdom. His hesitancy and the trials of conscience he underwent prior to that martyrdom have been much discussed, and he has been called a coward, but Rudolph Heinze in his article on Cranmer's life, "When I'm Weak, then I'm Strong," disagrees.

Cranmer accomplished a great deal in a short period of time. Although he held the archbishopric of Canterbury for over twenty years, for only five of those years was he given a free hand. Heinze argues that Cranmer's magnificent accomplishments and his courage exhibit the strengthening pattern of worship one finds in the Book of Common Prayer. That which he wrote to strengthen the church in England, strengthened him in the face of adversity.

Richard Hooker's work *The Laws of the Ecclesiastical Polity* is a great synthesis of patristic, medieval, and reformed theology, and the flower of the Elizabethan church. Roger Beckwith notes that while most Anglicans admire Richard Hooker more than they do Cranmer, in fact the *Laws* show that Hooker's theology of worship is fundamentally Cranmerian. The fifth book of the *Laws* expounds the theology of the Book of Common Prayer and consequently those who admire Hooker, whether Anglo-Catholic or evangelical, should also recognize that the Book of Common Prayer contains a theology not unique to Cranmer, but very much an expression of the church as a whole. It is a statement of reformed and catholic Christianity.

In these first three essays, the historical theology of sixteenth-century Anglicanism is presented. The latter three essays are directed to disputes about Cranmer's legacy. In "Recovering Confessional Anglicanism," Gillis

Harp makes a case for the continuing doctrinal importance of the Thirty-Nine Articles, despite arguments between evangelicals and Anglo-Catholics about their authority. He discusses a number of historical commentaries on the Articles which are excellent resources for better understanding them.

Ian Robinson addresses the complexities of Biblical interpretation from a literary standpoint by way of criticizing a celebrated literary treatment of the Bible written by Harold Bloom. Robinson argues that the Bible is one book, one coherent treatment of God and man. Although one may speak of the Bible as a single work with a coherent meaning, it is not coherent or a unity in quite the same way as is a poem, a work of historical research, or a mathematical equation. The Bible is a special case of unity; it is what the Apostles made of it under the guidance of the Holy Spirit and so methods and treatments of analysis must take that into account.

Turning to contemporary liturgical debate, Bryan Spinks' research into the history of liturgy shows that Dom Gregory Dix's book, *The Shape of the Liturgy* is based on a creative and not necessarily scholarly assertion about an ancient liturgical text that has turned out to be false. Dix took a document called the *Apostolic Tradition,* attributed to a shadowy figure named Hippolytus in second century Rome, and argued it was foundational to western liturgies. The influence of Dix's argument was immense, both on Vatican II and in Anglicanism. But it is clear that Dix's antagonism to the Reformation colored his research. As Professor Spinks remarks, the emphasis placed on Dix's work should be seen, in retrospect, as a scholarly fad, and certainly the *Apostolic Tradition* is no more 'authentic' a source than those that were available to Cranmer, who was no mean liturgical scholar in his own right.

A Brief Summary of Peter Toon's Life's Work

Peter Toon began his career as an historical theologian. In his first book *The Emergence of Hyper-Calvinism in English Nonconformity, 1689–1765,* he traced the transformation of Calvinist theology into its different branches: High Calvinism, Federal Theology, Antinomianism, and Arminianism. This research led Dr. Toon to publish further studies of the seventeenth century: *The Pilgrim's Faith* (1970) about the men and women who travelled to America on the Mayflower; *The Oxford Orations of John Owen* (1971), a translation of the works of that seventeenth-century Puritan theologian; and *God's Statesman* (1973) on the life and work of John Owen. Then, in

1973, Peter wrote *Puritans and Calvinism*. Studies of nineteenth-century evangelicalism were published in the following years. In the late 1970s, under the pressure of events, Dr. Toon turned his attention to defending matters of contemporary moment. Among the most notable of his efforts was *Let God be God* (1989), written with Bishop Graham Leonard, against the ordination of women. That work was written to explain and defend the coherence of biblical teaching, as found in the tradition of the Church, and repeated in the formularies of Anglicanism, such as the ordinal, and Book of Common Prayer. Peter Toon also wrote expositions of the Gospels and Epistles with his wife, Dr. Vita Toon. One may fairly say that his life's work serves to show how scriptural Anglicanism is in its origins, and how the rejection of, or ignorance about, the historical formularies of the Anglican Church, seems to have led to confusion about biblical orthodoxy. His final book, *A Foretaste of Heaven amidst Suffering,* written in his final months of life while suffering from amyloidosis, was published posthumously. This consideration of the last things illustrates the remarkable tenacity of his intellect, and his witness to the grace of God in the face of the shadows of death.

The Genesis of Modern Theology

Philosophers and theologians in Western Christendom have operated within a common orbit of ideas—in fact, it was only in the thirteenth and fourteenth centuries that philosophy and theology were distinguished as distinct disciplines of study. What is called "modern" philosophy and theology dates from the Enlightenment and may be identified loosely with the Cartesian turn in philosophy and the Newtonian revolution in science, when Christians came to think of faith as a matter of private choice rather than public affirmation, and philosophical and scientific reasoning as the only foundation for universal and objective truth. Such was not the case in the Middle Ages when most Christian theologians took the greatest works of ancient philosophy and literature to be examples of natural human reasoning at its very highest. The relationship between those works and the Christian faith was clearly articulated by Augustine in the *City of God* when he said that the wisdom of the ancients is a preparation for the Gospel, a *preparation evangelii*. It was understood by that statement that the ancients in the exercise of their natural reason had discovered the existence of the true God, although they had not known the fullness of his essential nature as revealed in Christ. A friendship between ancient philosophy and Christian theology continued into the later Middle Ages until divergent and contradictory interpretations of the Aristotelian metaphysical corpus drove Christian theologians into intense disagreement as to the usefulness of Aristotelian metaphysics to theology. In the course of this intellectual crisis the Western church divided.

Tracing the manner in which this philosophical crisis led to skepticism about the faith is a complex endeavor, and a topic of intense interest in the academy.[3] Generally it is spoken of as the Cartesian turn. In the sixteenth century Descartes renewed philosophical speculation; he argued that correctness in philosophical reasoning is entirely dependent upon method. In saying this he sent philosophy in a new direction. Descartes stated that one should not seek truth, as did the medieval thinkers, by speculating about the divinely created order, mounting by steps the vestiges of God in the world until reaching to God Himself, in the manner of a philosophical theologian such as St. Bonaventure. Instead the search for truth must begin by turning thoughts inward, looking for truth within the subjective, thinking self. He claimed that it was only by the methodological application of autonomous reason, and not the study of historical philosophy, that he was able to arrive at clear and distinct ideas as to what is true and what is untrue.

Descartes' philosophical approach to truth and to God was mirrored within theological circles. Luther wrote of the faith of the inner man; pietists intensified that idea; the Quakers spoke of the inner light of faith. Truth, religious and philosophical, became a matter of subjective knowledge and consequently a matter of contention.[4]

Cognitive dissonance, one might say, led eventually to skepticism about truth, and eventually skepticism as to the existence of God. Tracing the history of the steps by which we arrived at a modern world filled with angst, religious skepticism and a corresponding loss of confidence in the ability of human reasoning to attain to truth is complex. Today it can be

---

3. Charles Taylor's *A Secular Age,* which Peter Toon was reading in the last months of his life, is an attentive and careful discussion of the complex causes, and general characterstics of modern secularity. But one might construct a list of works both popular and scholarly on this topic beginning with C. S. Lewis, G. K. Chesterton, George Parkin Grant, Leo Strauss, Eric Voegelin, Richard Weaver, Alasdair MacIntyre, Jacques Maritain, and Walter Lippmann, none of whom present the same narrative, but all of whom recognize that in modernity there is not just a crisis of faith, but of the place of reason.

4. I speak here of Protestantism, although in Roman Catholicism the same trajectory of ideas was otherwise expressed.

said that reason itself has become a question. Are we reasoning creatures? If so, why do we not reason alike?[5] Are there not many truths? Is there meaning written into the lineaments of the universe? Can we know ourselves?

Anxiety about truth occurs at the same time that faith and religious practices, worship and doctrine have been relegated to the category of subjective, entirely personal choice for which no education can be regarded as necessary. It is commonly said that in the past people worshipped in a certain way because it fit their culture, and so today worship should fit our culture. Logically, of course, this manner of relegating all matters of religious practice to subjective choice implies the impossibility of attaining to a kind of intelligible and defensible true practice, and that is a problem if one is a Christian who desires to act in accord with the true faith. Furthermore the burden on the individual who seeks to argue that the practices and doctrine of the Church of England in the sixteenth century are good in and of themselves and of continuing value is very heavy. Entering into such a discussion requires that one question modern conceptions of the faith, and modern conceptions of reason, before defending those found in the historical received tradition. One must question the very presupposition that all ideas are culturally determined. One must show that the Book of Common Prayer was neither the projection of Cranmer's preferences nor an artifact unique to the sixteenth century, but consistent with the long and continuous practice of Christian worship, and therefore a very well-spring of Christian life. One might also need to show that it is different from the kinds of Christian prayer and worship that have developed in the last hundred years because it is consistent with historical practice.

Seminary Education Today

Seminary education in much of contemporary North American Anglicanism has been shaped by the categories of modern thought in the following ways: firstly, theology is often presented as culturally determined; secondly, theology which pre-dates modernity is neglected; and thirdly, it is assumed that different cultures cannot pray and worship in a common manner. In pursuit of cultural relevance, seminarians are encouraged to invent new liturgies in order to project their own faith experience into worship as a

5. Charles Taylor's *A Secular Age* describes this development. The problems presented to reasoning in the aftermath are described by Alasdair MacIntyre in his books *After Virtue,* and *Whose Justice, Which Rationality?*

means of making it more meaningful to themselves. Every connection to historical Anglican worship and doctrine is entirely extinguished. Among those who are interested in traditional liturgy, high and low church factions are inclined to argue over matters indifferent. The scriptural commentaries by the fathers of the early church and the works of sixteenth-century reforming theologians, all of which ought to be at the core of the curriculum, play a very small part. There are courses which introduce seminarians to Christian Marxism, feminism, and environmentalism, each advancing a particular interpretation of Christian experience, each with its plan for action. Seminarians are prepared to be social workers rather than teachers. Rival schools of biblical exegesis, each with its own epistemological assumptions, dominate biblical studies presenting students not with proof of the continuing veracity of the gospel, but interpretative chaos, all of which encourages an individual to express their faith in terms of subjective experience alone. *Praxis theology* makes a theoretical argument for that experience. All this unfortunately leaves seminarians tongue-tied if asked by parishioners to explain a point of doctrine.

Sixteenth-century English theologians read in the course of their studies a large and authoritative body of commentaries on Scripture, sermons, and treatises written over many centuries. This body of work had shaped and directed a continuous dialogue within the church as to the meaning of Biblical texts and doctrine. Cranmer knew he was working within a tradition of theological discourse and reasoning, and he sifted and discerned what was of greatest importance, disagreeing with some of the fathers of the church at some points, and agreeing with them at others. Submission to this tradition of study set parameters as to how Holy Writ was to be read within the church and offered a means by which to interpret the Bible.[6]

The magisterial Reformers of the sixteenth century inherited what in general terms might be called a framework for reading and praying the Bible. There was debate, there was disagreement, but in fifteen hundred years all possible orthodox and heterodox opinions had been canvassed. The objectivity offered by those texts and the subjectivity of the Christian theologian were united in the reception of the Word (through the Holy Spirit). This kind of education was not just bookish, abstract knowledge, but was of practical benefit *and* a means to grace. We pray and read so that we might reform our life and manners, as Cranmer in his *Preface to the Great Bible (1539–1540)* stated, drawing on the work of the fourth century

6. Null, "Thomas Cranmer and the Lively Word," 7–9.

saint Chrysostom. Until the Enlightenment there was a core curriculum. From this curriculum the Reformers inherited not so much a specific theology of the human soul, of nature and grace, secular and sacred authority, but texts crucial to those topics, and a way of approaching theology.

They also held an idea common to ancient and medieval ethics that godly habits of the soul are to a great degree determined by education, often from childhood; habits of prayer shape the intellect and will, and the content of the books a child reads teaches him how to distinguish good from bad, and teaches the merit of self-control.[7] Cranmer compiled the Book of Common Prayer not simply to act as a liturgy for the church, but to play the role of a magisterium in the church. It is the gospel set to prayer. It was written for families within the church; it was to guide parents in teaching their children the doctrine of the faith; and it was a means by which the family would participate within the body of Christ in the home if unable to attend a parish. It was not just for use of the clergy. It was to play a role in *formation of a Christian way of life* because being a Christian requires that one enter into a way of life lived under authority, the authority of the eternal gospel, taught one might hope by doctrinally learned bishops and priests who themselves recognize the authority of truth revealed and understood. Therefore to be Christian was to follow a way of life which combines prayer with study of doctrine and the reading of Scripture.

This picture of education as a pilgrimage of heart and mind, of habit and learning, has been lost. The Cartesian turn led Western Christians to place great importance, perhaps too great importance, on the subjective self as the only source of faith and truth.[8] As a result, Christians came to think of faith as a choice, a momentary subjective affirmation, for which nothing in life or learning could prepare them. Consequently historical theology became a matter of secondary importance, the practice of the faith neglected. Furthermore we tend to treat our religious beliefs as if they were a projection of our subjective self upon reality; our beliefs are an expression of who we are. Too few think that faith requires an openness to received doctrinal truths, or a life-long pilgrimage of prayer and historical and theological study. Yet, the irony is that we live in such ignorance, unlike our forebears, of the received truths of the faith, despite the fact that we have much easier

7. C. S. Lewis, entirely aware of this fact, treats of this view of education in a number of works, such as *The Abolition of Man*.

8. See Taylor, *Sources of the Self.*

access to texts of historical theology. Books are inexpensive, libraries are available. We ourselves stand in the way of knowing our own past.

In the sixteenth century Richard Hooker, the greatest of all Anglican theologians, confronted a church wherein there was intense and growing disputation as to the very nature and study of theology. The Puritans, or at least some of them, were skeptical about the relevance of past learning to present faith, and so Hooker found himself at the center of a great argument about the place of reason in relation to revelation. To paraphrase, Richard Hooker wrote that doctrine, theology, and worship, the laws of the church, are like a building or a tree, and what is invisible to the eye is of greater importance than what is visible. The *reasons* for the doctrines and laws of the church are buried deep, like the invisible foundations of a building which bear up its walls, like the roots of a tree which give the tree nourishment, they are more necessary than pleasant to look upon. Yet the pleasure taken from the walls and roof of a building, and from the shade of the tree, indeed our very enjoyment of the fruits of faith is entirely owed to what is hidden beneath, in the ground, out of sight. The purposes for why things are done and have been done within the church for centuries are buried deep, but yet they are the very source of its orthodoxy and life. Hooker wrote the *Laws of the Ecclesiastical Polity* so that men might not neglect the foundations of their faith for the enjoyment of current pleasures.[9] He would most certainly advise the same if speaking to the Anglican Church today.

Toon on Typologies of Contemporary Christianity

It was in an attempt to map the distance between the most important contemporary schools of theology and the Anglican formularies that Peter Toon wrote *The End of Liberal Theology: Contemporary Challenges to Evangelical Orthodoxy*. A "profound change in the Western appreciation of what is theology, how it is studied, and for what purpose it is pursued came about primarily because of the adoption of the principles of the Enlightenment within the universities of Europe . . . in the late eighteenth and early nineteenth century,"[10] he wrote. After reading a classic book on the sociology of religion by noted author Peter Berger,[11] an occasional contributor

9. Hooker, *Laws*, I.i.

10. Toon, *Liberal Theology*, xiv.

11. Peter Berger co-authored a couple of books with Richard John Neuhaus, at least one of which was read by Dr. Toon.

to Richard John Neuhaus' *First Things,* he decided to use Berger's[12] "typologies" to characterize the theological schools or ideas which are most influential.

Dr. Toon followed Berger in discussing modern religious consciousness. Berger had said that there is a "direct relationship between the cohesion of institutions and the subjective cohesiveness of beliefs, values, and worldviews."[13] He examined how each type of modern theology depends upon, and responds to, modern religious consciousness. Each type or school begins from within the standpoint of modern subjectivity, the modern awareness of the self, as the only means of knowing God because, as was indicated above, study of historical philosophy and theology are no longer part of the study of theology.

The essential difference between modern theology as described by Berger and Toon, and reformed and catholic theology found in the Book of Common Prayer and formularies is that the latter does not assume the autonomous self to be the starting point for discovery of religious belief, but rather that each individual discovers his true self through education in doctrine, and in prayer. Received doctrines held within the church appear to be alien to the modern subjective self who mistakenly thinks God is discovered in his own subjective experience. Therefore a very great and unbridgeable chasm appears to exist between belief, when presented as nothing more than a subjective affirmation of the faith, and objective received doctrine as expressed in the church. This chasm must be crossed for modern individuals to accept the Book of Common Prayer and formularies. Anglicans, Dr. Toon observed, should be aware that it is the emphasis on self-discovery, this individualism within modern consciousness which keeps Anglicans from accepting the traditional formularies. He also thought the Anglican way might prove a remedy to the chaos produced by this individualism.

According to Berger's thesis, as described in *The End of Liberal Theology,* the *Reductive* approach to Scripture, found in feminist theology or gay studies, accepts "the cognitive challenge of modernity," and tries to translate the truth of yesterday into terms more amenable to modern consciousness.[14] It entails *reducing,* in the sense of resolving or assimilating, scriptural imperatives to a particular program of action. Its defenders

12. Dr. Toon depended upon Peter Berger's *The Heretical Imperative: Contemporary Possibilities of Religious Affirmation.*

13. Berger, *Heretical Imperative,* 18.

14. Toon, *Liberal Theology,* 191.

say that Christians discover the faith where they are. Scripture, therefore, should be re-interpreted for modern consciousness. Reductive theology appears to be a bargain between modern consciousness and orthodox religious affirmations.

Rudolph Bultmann's theology of demythologization is paradigmatic of this model of theology. German theologian Rudolph Bultmann was among the most brilliant theologians of the mid-twentieth century; a friend of Heidegger, he objected to what he called the "mythological" character of orthodox theology because it is alien and alienating to contemporary, technologically attuned, secularized men and women. By myth he meant all tales of the miraculous in which the "otherworldly is represented as acting in this world."[15] For Christianity to suit the modern world and to take its place as a transformative force in contemporary life, it must be able to speak to men and women whose consciousness is formed by the conditions of modernity which are primarily technological, materialistic, and scientific. One can see that Anglicans who defend the ordination of women have in this manner *reduced* the fullness and complexity of scriptural teaching on women to modern awareness of equality.

At the other end of the spectrum is *Deductive* theology. This option affirms an unquestioned allegiance to moral and biblical norms of premodern times and takes the Bible to be the primary source of knowledge of the faith. The world, contemporary culture, and experience are perceived to be in tension with Biblical authority. Dr. Toon identified his own work as being more or less of this type. It is the dominant expression of Christian orthodoxy today. Frequently it is called "conservative" theology.

The Deductive option emerged in reaction to nineteenth-century liberal theology. The figure at its center is Swiss theologian Karl Barth. Barth's protestant and neo-orthodox followers thoroughly reject any bargain with modern consciousness. The world, contemporary culture, and modernity are seen to be in tension with the Bible, and so too much of historical theology on this account of its debt to ancient philosophy. This sets up a strong opposition between Scripture which is objectively true and subjective opinion and experience, whether individual or ecclesial. Religious doctrines are always *deduced*. "Whenever we hear or read such statements as 'the Bible says' and 'the Word of God states,' along with 'the church teaches' and 'tradition declares,' we are most probably encountering theology of the

---

15. Berger, *Heretical Imperative*, 102.

deductive type."[16] Deductive theology rejects experience in its entirety as a way to God. Yet the emphasis on objective, Biblical authority has no ground outside of the subjective self. Therefore it is a reaction against reductive and inductive forms of liberal theology without recourse to the doctrinal authority of the church and historical theological reasoning.

Thirdly, there is the *Inductive* approach, as exemplified by the work of German theologian Friedrich Schleiermacher. Inductive reasoning begins from the diversity of experience and abstracts from it, making generalizations, so to develop a hypothesis about the nature of reality. Inductive theology uses "the methods of the historian to uncover those human experiences that have become embodied in the various religious traditions."[17] It offers a method suitable to a sociologist of religion so it is unsurprising that Berger finds it useful, although one might say that theology and sociology in this model are not clearly distinguished. Berger wrote: "Properly understood faith and inductive reasoning stand in dialectical relationship to each other: I believe—and then I reflect about the implications of that fact; I gather evidence about that which is the object of my faith—and this evidence provides a further motive for believing."[18] Its synthetic tendency draws inspiration from the idea that the spirit moves in history, and so revelation is seen to be a continuing process. It too has little use for historical theology, except insofar as it is one aspect of a religious culture, it is one kind of evidence for believing. Berger's attachment to the Inductive model and to liberal Christian theology in general led him to assert that the history of Christianity is not the history of any particular theology, but of a particular kind of experience of the faith.[19]

Peter Toon noted that inductive theology had had an enormous impact on modern Anglican liturgies. *Lex orandi, lex credendi* (the law of praying is the law of believing) was taken out of context in order to argue that through the ritual of worship and singing we draw conclusions as to who God is,[20] so exalting the experience of prayer rather than the doctrinal formulations of the faith or the Gospel itself as the foundation of faith. The intention of modern liturgists was to change doctrine, or to make it secondary, by relying only upon the experience of worship and how they

16. Toon, *Liberal Theology*, 177.

17. Ibid., 183, quoting Berger, *Heretical Imperative*, 63.

18. Berger, *Heretical Imperative*, 143.

19. Berger, *Heretical Imperative*, 187.

20. Toon, *Liberal Theology*, 188.

think about God. Significantly, in the 1979 prayer book the Catechism was replaced by an "Outline of Faith" which begins not with God, but with human nature. This reflects an inductive approach to "discovering" the Trinity. As such, the study of theology as it existed historically in the sixteenth century and before, is of limited use. Once again subjective experience and objective doctrine are opposed.

Such a diverse group of theories, each of which can be identified with a particular view of the self, presents one with a series of questions: Does God direct the church, teach it and guide it primarily through subjective desires shaped by culture, or by a transformative consciousness of God revealed in our life and history? Or do we accept the truth as revealed once and for all in Christ as recorded in the Bible, and so reject all cultural and historical interpolations from experience as a ground for interpretation of Scripture? Upon recognizing the importance of these questions one must also ask: Is the truth of the faith subjective or objective? What importance should we place upon the culture around us, recognizing that it is through conversation and reading that our reasoning is honed and we develop in understanding and in faith? The typologies listed above offer incommensurable options—each depends upon a particular set of unquestioned presuppositions about the self, and each operates within a particular framework of ideas. There is no way to negotiate a middle ground or compromise position from which protagonists might engage in common discourse about matters of doctrine. There is no place for historical theology in the models of reasoning presented above.

Occasionally theologians of these schools may arrive at a common plan for action. By reasoning reductively or inductively one may come to approve of women's ordination, or of certain changes to the liturgy, albeit for very different reasons. So with many issues such as the ordination of practicing homosexuals, unity and division runs along political lines; unity exists for the sake of action. It has been remarked that Christians championing these radical doctrinal changes often do not recognize these issues as doctrinal. They are not able to express their ideas theologically. A plan of action therefore is seen as an end in itself.[21] This is the result of unexamined beliefs, values, and worldviews, indeed, the inability to convey whatever

21. Oliver O'Donovan made a similar point. In his research into the question of homosexuality in the Church of England, he noted that while there were many arguments made for the ordination of homosexuals and "gay" marriage, none rose to the level of a theological argument, within the traditional meaning of that term. See: *Church in Crisis: The Gay Controversy and the Anglican Communion*.

belief or value that one holds in theological terms. This is indicative of confusion about the place of reasoning in relation to matters of doctrine and faith.

A Revival of Anglican Way?

There is, as Peter Toon describes it, an interesting fourth alternative, sometimes called the Narrative school of theology.[22] On his reading, it need not conflict with Deductive theology and it might be seen to mitigate some of the weaknesses presented by the other types of theology, particularly their inability to negotiate Biblical truth and subjective experience. It looks to the Christian life to integrate subjective experience with received church doctrine. Peter Toon thought that properly understood Narrative Theology might be used to show that the historical Anglican Way is the only foundation for Anglicanism.

Theologians of the Narrative school have argued that the Bible is properly understood when it is read as an *interpretive framework for all reality,*[23] because the meaning of the Bible is learned within the church through worship and prayer. This is true to the Anglican tradition.[24] In this way the subjective experience of the individual Christian is interpreted in light of the gospel and the historical faith, in a community united in prayer and worship. In worship, in prayer, in participation of the sacraments, each individual joins in the whole Christian narrative, or otherwise put, the life of the church, the Body of Christ. Doctrine will be introduced, discussed, expounded and explained not as rationalistic and alien "talk about God, but [as] talk about the church's talk about God, salvation, and so on."[25]

The Cranmerian prayer book tradition was, of course, intended to provide such a narrative of meaning, although clearly Cranmer and the Reformers did not put it that way. By exhorting Christians to continual prayer and catechesis, by the daily offices, and Bible reading, and through

22. In his discussion of the Narrative school of theology, Dr. Toon depends upon Hans Frei's *Theology and Narrative: Selected Essays,* and George Lindbeck's, "Scripture, Consensus and Community," and *The Nature of Doctrine.*

23. Toon, *Liberal Theology,* 205, quoting Lindbeck.

24. The Archbishop of Canterbury, Rowan Williams, recently made this point with respect to Anglican worship. See his speech: *The Word of God in the Anglican Tradition,* 8 September, 2011.

25. Toon, *Liberal Theology,* 204,

the Homilies it offers a way by which an individual might ask and find answers to questions about the faith in such a way that the gospel, historical theology, and church history are integral to the answer.[26] The proclamation of the gospel is the role of the church, and in turn the church is guided by the formularies and historical teaching so that the individuals do not "leap," but rather receive the faith, in a manner by which it becomes true for them. In the Anglican way this requires participation in Morning and Evening Prayer according to order of the ecclesiastical seasons, the services of Baptism, Holy Communion, Marriage, Burial, and the entire cycle of daily life given in the Book of Common Prayer. That cycle unites Anglican Christians with Christians of the past as well as with other Anglicans today in a pattern of worship which dates from the early centuries of Christendom. It provides an interpretive framework for the gospel and theological content.

The modern autonomous self—shaped as it is by a culture of pluralism and by the continual pressure to choose—will find rest with God in the Book of Common Prayer because it offers more than a transitory Christian community; its cycle of worship places the worshipper within the larger narrative of the faith. Bible study and prayer groups do create community in modern churches, but given our mobility, and the fact that each group depends heavily upon the gifts of each member, they are a poor replacement for an order of worship and prayer and study which once united the entire communion. Peter Toon thoughtfully remarked that it is "the loss of narrative meaning, through the sole or excessive use of the deductive or inductive method, [that had] the effect of weakening the glue that holds the canon together."[27] Therefore, it is by "the reading of Scripture within the community of faith" that the Church can be renewed.[28] He hoped to persuade Anglicans that true renewal requires entering into the community of faith in worship within the Anglican way.

In concluding *The End of Liberal Theology*, Dr. Toon remarked that evangelical and otherwise orthodox Anglicans have "mistakenly held that

---

26. Alasdair MacIntyre has argued that each life can only be understood in light of whatever larger narrative to which they belong. There is no life which is not informed by some *telos* or end which offers meaning. Reason is therefore a means by which to negotiate rival and incommensurate goods. He argued that the Aristotelian, or teleological model of reason is therefore superior to other models because it offers a way to negotiate the problems raised by other models of rationality. See MacIntyre, *After Virtue*.

27. Toon, *Liberal Theology*, 206.

28. Ibid., 207.

[the] challenge is only the area of ideas."[29] Evangelicals particularly "have not reckoned with the fact that ideas do not succeed in history and culture because of their truthfulness but because of their inter-relationship to social processes. . . . If modernity . . . is a social reality and a global culture created by capitalism, technology, and information, then it is possible to resist the ideas of modernity and still be caught up in the social processes."[30] While many conservative Christians openly criticize the secularizing aspects of modernity, they adopt a subjective and experiential order of prayer which they think more Biblical than the Book of Common Prayer. In reality they are simply reflecting modern consciousness in their liturgy.

By using the Book of Common Prayer, it is possible to join the church universal, the historic Christian church, in a form which is both reformed and catholic. The Anglican way requires study of history and historical theology, attention to received doctrine, and submission to ordered prayer, but it results in better comprehension of the faith, and may mitigate against the kind of errors about which Richard Hooker warned many centuries ago. The way of the Christian pilgrim is unchanging from generation to generation.

Conclusion

Since the Episcopal Church in the United States rejected the fullness of Anglican theology as expressed in the historic Book of Common Prayer and the formularies it has been neither reformed nor catholic. As disunity is the result of epistemological and theological confusion, unity will be regained in common learning and prayer. Without renewal from within the practices and theology of the universal church the communion cannot be repaired. The life of the mind and the conversion of the heart will occur together.

It is not simply the loss of learning, but the loss of Cranmer's vision of a godly and Christian order of living which Peter Toon identified as the primary weakness in Anglicanism today. Theological confusion and moral error are symptomatic of not acknowledging that the Christian life is a pilgrimage wherein one forms an *ethos*, a habit of prayer and worship through the reading of Scripture in a manner passed down through the centuries to Cranmer. There are certain doctrines that must be believed for one to be

29. Ibid., 212.
30. Ibid.

saved. These are found in the gospel of Christ and detailed in the creeds. The Christian life entails expressing those doctrines in prayer *and* mind.

Augustine of Hippo began the *Confessions* by observing the following: "Grant me, Lord to know and understand whether a man is first to pray to you for help or to praise you, and whether he must know you before he can call you to his aid. If he does not know you, how can he pray to you?" The conclusion which he drew was that prayer and knowledge, through the grace of God, are inseparable because both belong to Faith. Augustine added: "The thought of you stirs him so deeply that he cannot be content unless he praises you, because you made us for yourself and our hearts find no peace until they rest in you." The Anglican way is Augustinian in its appreciation of the continual interplay of heart and mind and grace in the formation of the intellect and will, all renewing and fulfilling that internal, created, desire to love God. The Book of Common Prayer makes praise of God the first duty in the morning and the last duty at the end of day; it offers prayers for the beginning of life and its end. It instructs men how to live as Christians both catholic and reformed. From his early works of intellectual history to *A Foretaste of Heaven amidst Suffering,* Anglicanism is described as catholic and reformed, and Dr. Toon was in his life and thought an example of the Christian pilgrim seeking the truth of the faith through a life ordered to prayer, learning, and the reading of Scripture, the Anglican way.

1

In Memoriam Peter Toon: Sermon Delivered at the Memorial Service

Friday July 24, 2009

All Saints' Church, Wynnewood, Pennsylvania

REV. GRAHAM EGLINGTON

For none of us liveth to himself, and no man dieth to himself. For whether we live, we live unto the Lord; and whether we die, we die unto the Lord; whether we live, therefore, or die, we are the Lord's. For to this end Christ both died and rose, and revived, that he might be Lord both of the dead and the living.

ROMANS 14:7–9

One of my goddaughters is a star University league basketball player in Canada. When I explained to her what I was to be about this afternoon, and my trepidation, her response was not encouraging. She hardly hesitated before saying that it would be like her playing in an exhibition match in front of an audience of NBA players. Alas, too true, too true, as the first Duke of Cambridge, sixth son of George III, was wont to interject during divine service. But, I have been chosen. I can but plead a long association and a close friendship with our dear brother Peter, and long years with him at the Front. As a keen student of the American culture in which he lived, Peter would understand about playing before the NBA assembled. I trust that you will also, and forbear, especially as it is not given to many to be as incisive and brief as Peter.

I have approached my task this afternoon deeply sensible of the kindness Peter showed to so many of us, and of his concern for the welfare of his friends and acquaintances, and not them alone, but his adversaries in controversy also. Peter took what he did and his personal relations seriously, but never himself, and his kindness and gentle humour were rarely concealed. The sense of loss and of mourning about this occasion is dreadfully real for Vita, and for Deborah, and for many others also whose lives were touched, enhanced, enlivened, and above all edified by our beloved friend, not least your poor preacher.

I am also deeply sensible of the responsibility that falls to me to say something of substance worthy of the brilliant, learned, competent, articulate, and kindly man, devoted champion of the Anglican Way, and faithful Christian we remember today. Though the battle-front to which Peter had been called in recent decades was the Anglican Way, he well understood that the essential thing was that he was a Christian. Peter walked with his hand in that of the Lord Jesus. He knew and understood fully that salvation comes not from the Anglican Way, but by acceptance of Jesus. He had a full and complete understanding of our Gospel lesson that though mankind is given as one gift to the Son, yet each man and woman must come to Jesus. None shall perish who seek life in the Bread of Life. Peter fully accepted the corollary of this saving gift. All who are Christians make themselves God's servants. Christ purchased Peter's salvation by his death and resurrection, and Peter entered his service unreservedly, placing his formidable talents fully in the Lord's service. Whether, therefore, Peter lived or died, and in everything that he did, he did it for the Lord as part of the service he owed, and out of an abundance of love. And a good and faithful servant he proved himself to be.

Peter is so well known to those of us present today that someone will say, even though this be a Memorial Service and not a funeral, that there is no need to rehearse his qualities. And another may feel impelled to remind me what a horror Peter had of eulogies at funerals. But we are not here today to bury Peter, nor yet simply to praise him. We are here to remember him and to be edified by his life and work, and to draw from them lessons for building up the body of Christ, the very thing which was Peter's mission and for which he understood the Anglican Way to be so well suited for so many, if only it were properly understood and followed. His life and work afford lessons we should be earnest to identify, to learn from and to make practical use of. Yet, there is something more sublime even than that. We who are here today, and so many others, are drawn "as seedlings around a watercourse"[1] to a godly, noble, good, kind, humble, and effective man. Peter did not live to himself, nor yet did he die to himself. "People do detect goodness in others, and they respond," and so often by putting forth their best in the situations in which God has placed them. It is true that in this world there is ingratitude and jealousy, to which Peter was no stranger, and it is equally true that virtue, as also competence and clarity of thought and expression, can often be lonely, but "when a person rings true, many can hear, and they do respond. Nobility of soul echoes first from other souls."

Beloved, our response to Peter's life and death cannot be limited to our attendance here, or to prayers by those others in this vast continental empire and beyond who would wish to be with us but who cannot practicably be so.

Peter lived to the edifiying of the church, and in death he leaves us as heirs of a great legacy which can be used for the same purpose. He was not unsuccessful in what he was about. Conjure with where the Anglican Way would be now in North America had he not lived and worked amongst us. And work he did, tirelessly, selflessly. His written output alone was of Stakhanovite proportions. And how he wrote; with what clarity, simplicity and directness, and above all courage. There was no fudge, for Peter did have an unerring instinct for the essence of any matter, something which made many fellow travellers in the conservative and traditional paths uncomfortable. His writings, from books to email tracts are models of accessibility, an invaluable legacy and resource for those who are left to champion the Anglican Way. His contacts and reaching out to others who did not fully realize the centrality of the use of the classical Books of Common Prayer to that Way must not be lost or ignored. By the grace of God Peter was the conscience, and the beating heart, of the Anglican Way on this continent. God's grace was not bestowed on him in vain. He laboured perhaps more

1. This and the following quotations in this paragraph are taken from Matthew Parris, "A funeral teaches me that Gray was wrong in his Elegy about the loneliness of virtue." This piece, in the *Another Voice* series in *The Spectator*, contains a train of thought remarkably appropriate to the late Peter Toon, and was even more remarkably published within a fortnight of his death.

abundantly than anyone for the Anglican Way, and yet, as he would echo St. Paul, not he, but the grace of God working in him. This modern apostle did it all through setbacks, adversities, personal disappointments, betrayals, persecution, elitist condescension, and wearying journeys, meeting calls for assistance from all corners and all comers.

By God's grace also we shall not let his legacy and the corpus of his written work be effaced. They must be used by us for the spiritual building up of individual Christians and of the church. These special gifts that fall to us could, of course, be appropriated individualistically, but, beloved, that would be quite wrong. They must be shared with the whole church. Peter did not live to himself or even to a select few. He shared everything and gave of himself to all, whether they appreciated it, or not. It is up to us to ensure that Peter has not died only to himself and his Lord, and to those who mourn him personally. His legacy must be shared. That it seems to me is the peculiar responsibility of the Society which has gathered us together today, and of its sister societies abroad.

One aspect of Peter's work and legacy in particular should be our constant study. He was an avid student of the culture in which he had come to live and work, and in which he found his mission. He was assisted—his study was facilitated—by his familiarity with so many cultures in which Anglicanism is to be found, from the English Evangelical to the African and the Australian. There can have been few persons living with such a wealth of experience and knowledge of the Anglican Diaspora. But it was his determination to engage with the culture and the social and religious imaginaries of these United States I wish to notice now. He was a constant student, a keenly observant participant in the contemporary, and a deeply reflective commentator. The longer he lived here, the more deeply he penetrated the imaginary and the culture of religious choice of America. Peter, as must we, began with the premise that the Anglican Way of the formularies and the use of the classical Books of Common Prayer was and is an authentic expression of the catholic faith, and not some wishy-washy and transient "middle way." Many in recent times have concluded otherwise, and have turned to other jurisdictions in order to anchor themselves in the catholic faith. Peter always wished them well. The next question Peter grappled with, as must we, is this: is the Anglican Way a viable expression of the catholic faith in the United States? This same question is critical in both Canada and Australia. Many, including those in command of the institutional Anglican churches, have concluded that the Anglican Way is not viable in these three countries. Many have followed those commanders into a new dwelling place, while others have joined the principled exodus elsewhere. And yet others remain holed up in precarious peculiars. It was the issue of viability which exercised Peter's holy imagination so much, and it is why he studied the culture so carefully, and why he so relentlessly distinguished, and with such great precision, the efforts of those who wished to argue for viability by changing the Anglican Way, or by using it for particular campaigns, or by diluting it, but to some lesser extent than had those in command of the institutional churches.

Beloved, it is this question of viability which we have to address for the benefit of others. It is the demonstration of this viability which is our task. Not in the sense of finding a way to maintain the Anglican Way for ourselves, but in the sense of finding and prosecuting the means to make the Anglican Way relevant to the spiritual needs and searches of others. We are, despite that challenge, which is really a quest, *dwellers*, to use the current terminology.[2] We are one of the centres of traditional religious authority and practice in the contemporary world. We dwell in a different place than do those who dwell in the contemporary Western Anglican churches, but we are dwellers nonetheless. Outside, in the culture, there is a zone inhabited by folk of Christian, even Anglican, recollection who might be touched in their own quest for something beyond self-authenticity or who may find their authenticity completed in the Anglican Way. And there are others who practise a minimalist religion in their immediate circle of family and friends, honouring God in the particular people who share their lives. Peter was very alert to the potential amongst such folk for the use of the Common Prayer as a devotional tool and as a portal to the catholic faith through the Anglican Way. But far, far greater, and especially so in Canada and in Australia, are the number of those potential seekers who have no Anglican recollection, no Christian connection or memory, and no comprehension of religious language or concepts whatever—those whose default position is the atheistic presupposition of our time, of our elites and of the intelligentsia. They look at the church as the Nazarenes looked at our Lord; they cannot conceive of her as being of use or as having a future. And then there are those who are simply antagonistic to religion, to the authority forms of the past from which they see themselves as having escaped in

---

2. The terms "dwellers/dwelling" and "seekers/seeking" are attributed to Robert Wuthnow, *After Heaven*, ch. 1, and have been used extensively by Charles Taylor in his *A Secular Age*.

order to achieve authenticity, whether described as self-fulfilment, or otherwise. They look upon the church as evil, riddled with sexual and financial corruption, and bent on repression.

Peter did not, alas, have the opportunity to grapple fully with Charles Taylor's vast new work, *A Secular Age*,[3] which despite all the criticisms of it I have heard nonetheless contains most useful empirical insights and helpful categories. These allow one to identify the very significant differences between the culture and religious imaginary of the USA and those of, for example, Australia and Canada, and the differences in terms of religion between the contemporary imaginaries of Australia and Canada. A study of Taylor's work shows, I suggest, just how prescient Peter's far more accessible writing was, and just how much it is brought into relief by Taylor's analyses, as is Michael Hogan's writing in Australia in the 1980s.[4] For Peter *had* come to fasten his attention on those who seek something beyond themselves, just as, to be fair, the institutional churches had already done. It was Peter's conclusion that the Institutional Way was an essentially empty way, and that the Anglican Way had a future as an offer of substance and hope to some who sought after the transcendent beyond the freedom and self-expression which are the prevailing characteristics of our culture, and which are not to be dismissed as evil.

The working out of this conclusion was occupying Peter through much of his writing. It is what must occupy us if we accept the authenticity of the Anglican Way, and that it is viable into the future. In doing so we must acknowledge that the Anglican Way has its drawbacks, its baggage to use the modern idiom, in this country and in parts of Canada and Australia—its Englishness in expression and history; its long connection with authority and the formerly ruling elites in Canada and Australia; the fact that liturgical religion, and liturgical Christianity in particular, is at a deep discount in the culture of equality and individualism. Then there is the Anglican Way's supposed place as part of the enchanted world of a superstitious, irrational, and unscientific past; its tendency to seek unchallengeable authority, either in a rigid Episcopal despotism or a literal reading of the Bible; its tendency to reduce to the cold rationalism of propositional revelation, on the one hand, or into clericalism, ritualism, and gay colonization on the other. And crucially there is its previous default position, or major and influential

3. Taylor, *A Secular Age*. The concepts of authenticity and self-authenticity are discussed at length in chs. 13 and 14.

4. Hogan, *Sectarian Strand*.

default position, in all the North Atlantic and Australasian countries. And all this no matter that these same factors, bar one, are no drawback in West and East Africa. And that one factor may be determinative. In Africa the Anglican Way is not a previous default position of the population. It is for so many a new and exciting way to God, to forgiveness and to hope. Peter was very wise to put so much emphasis on Africa, and to try, albeit with limited success, to interest the several Prayer Book Societies in filling the hungry demand for Prayer Books in that continent, so that the Anglican Way might flourish where it is actually sought after. It is that hunger for and excitement by the gospel that we need to bring back to mind and to show forth to seekers, though they may initially be thinking in vaguer terms of "aspiring to a transformation that goes beyond human flourishing."[5]

Peter's life and work bids us identify the seekers who may be assisted and to work out how to assist them. We are not a club for those I call the PLU's—the people like us—for we shall all be gone in the twinkling of an eye, and palliative spiritual care is but one aspect of the catholic faith and not a definition of it. We are not a reflection of a political expression in the state or of some past ascendancy. We are not part of a tribal totem. We are not the religious counterpart to the Gilbert and Sullivan operas Peter loved so well. Peter *taught* us these things and in so doing he created a movement which can, with God's prevenient grace, reach out to seekers. Peter saw the need to embrace those, particularly in the recent exodus out of the institutional churches, for whom the traditional religious register of our language was a stumbling block. He saw the need for groups of dwellers in the Anglican Way to remain together in different circumstances, and in enterprising ways. For if the seekers are to find the gospel, there must be dwellers to assist and interest them. He spent countless hours in explaining the Anglican Way to those who sought it, however tangentially, and to those who thought they were already in it simply by adoption of a brand name. He never ceased to reach out. And though he did not use the current terms of dwellers and seekers I have employed, he constantly sought the seekers and was above all patient with them, seeking himself at all times to understand the land where for the nonce they dwelt.

That beloved is *our* mission. There is no future in the midst of the circled wagons. Equally, there is no Anglican future in the suppression of the Anglican Way as thoroughly as the Constantinople clergy suppressed Old Russia. The call to us, and to all North American Christians is, in Peter's

5. Taylor, *A Secular Age,* 510.

words one week before he died, nothing less than "the re-establishment in the human mind and in public worship of the biblical narrative and of its great themes of Creation, Redemption and Judgment, and the full place and perfection of Jesus Christ in the divine everlasting redemptive work. The simplest yet demanding way of growth into this mindset and ethos is the recovery of and taking seriously of the Common Prayer of the Church. . . . The regeneration of Anglican Christianity will never occur without the dynamic recovery of the Common Prayer."[6]

The oft quoted words of John Donne reflect with great poignancy our state this afternoon: "Any man's death diminishes me because I am involved in mankind, and therefore never need to learn for whom the bell tolls: it tolls for me." All of us present, and especially Vita and Deborah, have been diminished in various ways and on different levels by Peter's death. And Vita and Deborah like human beings from time immemorial bear the pain of grief and profound sorrow. As we express our sympathy to them, and thank Almighty God for all that Peter was enabled to do and to be, and for the precious bequest he leaves to us, we thank Vita and Deborah for sharing Peter with us. The sacrifices involved for them in so active and productive, yet chequered, a life only they can know. Our profound gratitude they should know also.

And now, beloved, we come to that true equality which comes in eternity, for we shall all die, and we shall all be raised.

I, and all of us, can say of Peter: We shall remember you until the Resurrection, in love, in gratitude, and in respect. Through God's mercy and providence you have left us with so great a legacy for building up the body of Christ. While we live we pledge to follow your admonition: We *will* press on. And we pray that when *we* shall have been gathered to our fathers, and then raised and accounted righteous as washed in the Blood of the Lamb, we shall join you in God's holy place, in glory everlasting.

For whether we live, we live unto the Lord: and whether we die, we die unto the Lord; whether we live therefore or die, we are the Lord's.

> *Low before Him with our praises we fall,*
> *Of whom, and in whom, and through whom are all;*
> *Of whom, the Father; and in whom, the Son;*
> *Through whom, the Spirit, with them ever one. Amen.*[7]

6. Email from Peter Toon to David Virtue, "Spirituality, Devotion, Piety and Godliness and Sanctifying," April 17, 2009.

7. Final stanzas of *O quanta qualia*, Peter Abelard, translated by J. M. Neale.

I heard a voice from heaven, saying unto me, Write, From hence-
forth blessed are the dead which die in the Lord: Even so, saith the
Spirit, for they rest from their labours.
Revelation 14:13

2

"When I'm Weak then I'm Strong": Thomas Cranmer's Struggle to Establish the Anglican Way

DR. RUDOLPH W. HEINZE

In his 1983 study of Anglicanism, entitled *The Anglican Way*, Peter Toon summarized the essence of Anglicanism as follows:

> The Episcopal Church is called to be both evangelical and catholic. In other words, the call of God to the Episcopal Church in these times, when the one Church of God is sadly divided, is that it should be simultaneously evangelical and catholic. This does not mean that she is to be evangelical in her preaching and catholic in her liturgy. It is not a matter of being sometimes evangelical and sometimes catholic. The Church is called to be catholic and evangelical all the time in all that she is and does.[1]

In a work which remains one of the best brief summaries of the essential beliefs of the Anglican Communion for the laity, Dr. Toon described in less than a hundred pages what it meant to be both "catholic and evangelical all the time." Throughout his ministry he struggled to impress this vision of Anglicanism on the wider Anglican community, and was a spokesman

1. Toon, *Anglican Way*, 11.

for authentic Anglicanism in contrast to those who are sometimes more committed to party loyalties and the beliefs associated with those traditions rather than historic Anglicanism. As might be expected, in order to describe the essential beliefs of the Anglican Communion, Dr. Toon relied extensively on the Anglican formularies,[2] which owe so much to the genius of Archbishop Thomas Cranmer. Dr. Toon was a great admirer of the first Anglican archbishop and he has been a persistent spokesman for preserving Cranmer's heritage in the modern church. Consequently, it seems fitting to include an essay exploring some aspects of Cranmer's ministry in a memorial volume dedicated to Peter Toon.

Although Cranmer's contribution to the Anglican tradition is almost universally acknowledged,[3] it is not always recognized how little time he had to establish his understanding of biblical Christianity in the Church of England and how much opposition he faced. His struggle to establish a church in England which conformed to the teachings of Holy Scripture and that was both evangelical and catholic was often a lonely one in which he was sometimes even opposed by fellow evangelicals. Yet it is hard to imagine a more productive life than Cranmer's. He was not only the genius behind the Book of Common Prayer and the Ordinal, but he also produced an Anglican statement of faith which is the basis of our present Thirty-Nine Articles. In addition, he played a major role in making a vernacular translation of Scripture available to the English people and wrote many of the homilies which were so significant in communicating the evangelical faith to the English church.

These are only a few of the major accomplishments of a man who spent most of his ministry confronting serious opposition. Cranmer was

---

2. See for example his summary statement in the chapter entitled "The Anglican Experience." "The Thirty-Nine Articles of Religion state the faithfulness of the Church of England to Scripture and true Catholic tradition. The Book of Homilies illustrates in sermon form what reformed Catholicity means for people in the pews. The Book of Common Prayer provides services of worship which teach Scriptural doctrines through revised, traditional forms, and the Ordinal contains services for the consecration of a bishop, the ordination of a priest and the making of a deacon." Toon, *Anglican Way,* 69.

3. Even those who might not fully sympathize with the evangelical understanding of Cranmer's contribution to Anglicanism recognized and commended Cranmer's contribution to Anglicanism. For example, Colin Dunlop, the Dean of Lincoln Cathedral, who preached the sermon commemorating the 400th anniversary of Cranmer's martyrdom in 1956, stated that it was Cranmer "more definitely than any other single man, who moulded even if unconsciously, the character of Anglicanism." Dunlop, *Thomas Cranmer,* 6.

Archbishop of Canterbury from 1533 to 1555. During those twenty-two years he had approximately five years in which he was free to lead the Church of England in the direction he considered the correct God-ordained path. He was in his late fifties when he had his first real opportunity to introduce the type of theology and worship to the Church of England that he believed was true to the teaching of Holy Scripture. Even during those years he faced opposition. In the last two years of Edward VI's reign others had the ear of the political leaders to the degree that Cranmer had to accept changes he did not consider proper. In order to accomplish his goals, Cranmer often had to make what could be considered moral compromises; consequently, some historians, especially those who do not sympathize with his theological beliefs, have portrayed Cranmer as a coward or a sycophant who supported his monarch's often morally questionable policies for personal gain.[4]

Until recently even Cranmer's sympathetic biographers did not always present their subject in a universally favorable manner.[5] The review of Diarmaid MacCulloch's new biography of Cranmer[6] in *The Times* began with the statement, "Cranmer is nobody's hero."[7] Although as with all sweeping generalizations it clearly is an inaccurate statement, Cranmer has not been as much of a "hero" among Anglicans as other reformers are to their modern day followers. Thus the lack of attention given to the Cranmer quincentenary in 1989 compared to the attention given to Luther in 1983 and Zwingli in 1984 is not surprising.[8] For some in the Church of England Cranmer is, in fact, more of an embarrassment than a hero, and the

---

4. "His [Cranmer's] life was the life of a cowardly time-serving hypocrite, a perjured person and a traitor," *The Saturday Review,* 25 July, 1860, 123. Cited in Null, *Cranmer's Doctrine,* 2; Brooks, *Cranmer in Context,* 117ff., includes brief selections from both negative and positive interpretations of Cranmer's life and works. See also Ridley, *Thomas Cranmer* for a discussion of the Cranmer historiography.

5. See for example Ridley's closing assessment of Cranmer. Ridley, *Thomas Cranmer,* 410–11.

6. MacCulloch, *Cranmer.*

7. Ackroyd, "He Followed the King's Devices and Desires," 38.

8. A few scholarly conferences were devoted to Cranmer studies, the British Library set up a Cranmer exhibition and the Archbishop of Canterbury gave a commemorative lecture at Lambeth Palace. If Peter Newman Brooks had not written his *Cranmer in Context*, the quincentennial year might have passed without a major new publication on Cranmer. Even the Post Office, which will normally produce commemorative stamps for the slightest excuse, ignored the Cranmer anniversary despite his massive impact on English culture and the English language through the Book of Common Prayer and the *Homilies.*

commemorative article in the *Church Times* was considerably more critical than complimentary. Statements such as "he was not a complete coward"[9] do not particularly enhance Cranmer's reputation. Even those scholars who tried to find good things to say about Cranmer, like the Swiss Protestant Merle d'Aubigne, did not emphasize his tenacity in the face of challenges. Rather he noted that it was very different qualities which preserved Cranmer's life and enabled him to do his work. "The extreme prudence of Cranmer, his timidity, his want of decision, his pliability, deplorable in certain cases preserved him under the government of the despotic Tudor . . . and thus saved, with his own life, the work for which he was required."[10]

Fortunately, since the quincentenary, Cranmer has received a more balanced and positive assessment in Diarmaid MacCulloch's massive new biography. In addition, Cranmer was fittingly honored on the 450th anniversary of his martyrdom in 2006. A special service was held at the university church of St. Mary the Virgin in Oxford, the site of Cranmer's final trial, using his liturgy in the Book of Common Prayer. Following the service, in which the Archbishop of Canterbury preached, the congregation processed to the iron cross in Broad Street that marks the site of Cranmer's martyrdom and the account of Cranmer's death was read. The procession then continued on to the Martyr's Memorial where Dr. Toon read the Gospel and Archbishop Williams laid a wreath. At one point in his sermon the Archbishop called Cranmer "a constitutionally timid man struggling to be brave,"[11] and although this was a reference to a specific incident in Cranmer's life,[12] this description could be applied generally; it is remarkable what this "timid man" accomplished in the face of fierce opposition.

Cranmer's accomplishments provide graphic proof of what can be achieved by persistent and patient work even in the face of powerful opposition,[13] but a number of questions come to mind when considering

9. Edwards, "Faith with Thanksgiving," 11.

10. Merle D'Aubinge, *Vindication of Cranmer's Character*, 9.

11. Williams, "The Archbishop of Canterbury's Sermon," 8.

12. The full statement was: "When he [Cranmer] wrote to King Henry in unhopeful defense of Anne Boleyn and Thomas Cromwell, the convoluted sentences and sentiments show not only a constitutionally timid man struggling to be brave (and all the braver for that), but a man uncomfortably capable of believing himself deceived and of seeing the world in double perspective." Williams, "The Archbishop of Canterbury's Sermon," 8.

13. Null states that: "Thomas Cranmer devoted the full powers of his position as Primate of All England to inculcating the Protestant faith into every fiber of English life and law. In doing so he shattered forever medieval Catholicism's hegemony over English society." Null, *Cranmer's Doctrine*, 1.

the struggles Cranmer underwent in the course of his ministry. They include: How did this timid man manage to endure in the face of so many obstacles, painful experiences, and disappointments? How did he manage to continue his struggle to change the English church so that it conformed to what he considered the teaching of the Scripture? How did he survive the final test of his work and his faith in Mary's reign? To use the words of the Apostle Paul, why did he not "lose heart"[14] in the face of the opposition, disappointments, and distressing events he experienced? Unfortunately, it is very difficult for the historian to penetrate into Cranmer's inner being in order to know for certain how he dealt with the challenges confronting him because he was a very private man who never revealed his deepest feelings and fears except to his closest friends and associates. In dramatic contrast to Luther, who did not hesitate to discuss his most personal struggles in his letters and writings, and who wrote extensively about his wife and family, Cranmer never commented much on his personal life. For example, there is only one mention of his second wife and children in his three hundred surviving letters. One of the men who knew him best, his servant and early biographer Ralph Morice wrote:

> He was a man of such temperature of nature, or rather so mortified, that no manner of prosperity or adversity could alter or change his accustomed conditions; for, being the storms never so terrible or odious, nor the prosperous estate of the time never so pleasant, joyous or acceptable, to the face of the world his countenance, diet or sleep commonly never altered or changed, so that they which were most nearest and conversant about him, never or seldom perceived by no sign or token of countenance, how the affairs of the prince or the realm went. Notwithstanding, privately with his secret and special friends, he would shed forth many bitter tears, lamenting the miseries and calamities of the world.[15]

As MacCulloch points out "those friends have not betrayed their confidence and Cranmer's private face remains for the most part inscrutable."[16] There is, however, some evidence in Cranmer's writings that enable us to get behind that outward mask of tranquility, and which helps us to understand how he managed to survive with his faith intact even in the worst times of his life. Before turning to that subject it is necessary to comment

14. 2 Cor 4:1.

15. Nichols, *Narratives of the Days of the Reformation*, 244.

16. MacCulloch, *Cranmer*, 1.

on some of Cranmer's other personality characteristics and to summarize the events of his life so we can better understand the challenges he faced and how he reacted to them.

One of Cranmer's characteristics that helps to explain his reaction to different situations was his scholarly approach to problems. Cranmer was first and foremost a scholar. He spent well over half his adult life at the University of Cambridge. He did not leave the University until he was in his mid-forties and his scholarly approach never left him. Unfortunately, it helped to undermine his ability to stand firm in the last months of his life. As a scholar he was always aware of the arguments of the opposition, and that sometimes made it difficult to stand firm when a decisive statement was needed. Nevertheless, when he did arrive at a position, it was the result of ripe deliberation and carefully weighing possible options. Although Cranmer always had a deep commitment to the Holy Scriptures, and as a university examiner he would not allow students to take their degree if they were ignorant in biblical studies, he was more conservative in his theological views than many of his university colleagues. He was even critical of Luther's views when he first came into contact with them. Furthermore, there is no evidence that he was initially sympathetic to, or that he met with, those early English Protestants who gathered regularly in the White Horse Tavern in Cambridge to discuss the new theology.

Another personality characteristic of Cranmer that has been widely recognized by his biographers was his gentle spirit. In contrast to the more robust and outspoken reformers like Luther and Knox, Cranmer was a gentle man who preferred peace to conflict, and certainly would have preferred unity among Christians rather than the deep divisions that developed as a result of the Reformation. He tried very hard to bring unity among Protestants and was especially grieved about the divisions over the Eucharist. While the Roman Catholic Council of Trent was meeting to define Catholic doctrine in opposition to Protestantism, Cranmer wrote letters to Protestant leaders Bullinger, Melanchthon, and Calvin, inviting them to come to England for a conference in order to unite Protestants.[17] He was, however, unsuccessful. A final characteristic of Thomas Cranmer was his deep commitment to the monarchy and especially Henry VIII. He was a devoted servant of the King throughout Henry's reign. Even when he disagreed with Henry's actions and when his theology had begun to differ from his monarch's beliefs, he still continued to serve the King loyally.

17. Cranmer, *Works,* II, ed. Cox, 216.

Before he entered the King's service Cranmer was a relatively unknown and unimportant person. Born in the obscure Nottinghamshire village of Aslocton, he was the second son of a small landholder. After his father's death in 1501, his mother sent him to Cambridge where he spent twenty-one happy years. He received his doctorate in 1523 and settled down to the pleasant life of a university lecturer. As pointed out earlier, even though he had a deep commitment to Scripture and was most likely a conservative humanist, there is no indication that he was attracted to the beliefs of the continental Reformation or that he participated in the discussions in the White Horse Tavern. Although he did not have any really outstanding accomplishments and did not publish any major works, he clearly was a competent teacher and scholar, and was well respected at Jesus College where he held a fellowship.

He might well have spent the remainder of his life in the University,[18] had he not been asked to serve as a diplomat in the king's service and become involved in what was called the "king's great matter," which simply meant Henry VIII's effort to annul his first marriage to Catherine of Aragon. In August 1529, as the result of a chance meeting with two former Cambridge classmates, Dr. Stephen Gardiner and Dr. Edward Foxe, who were now in the King's service, Cranmer's life was radically changed. At that meeting Cranmer made the suggestion that the impasse which had been reached in the King's efforts to annul his first marriage might best be resolved by a general canvassing of university theologians throughout Europe. Cranmer's idea was neither new nor effective since scholars at universities were in the final analysis more influenced by political loyalties than the evidence of their disciplines, but like a true academic Cranmer hoped that truth would emerge from his discipline. It was that suggestion which led Henry VIII to summon him to London and Cranmer now entered the King's service, eventually becoming his Ambassador to the German Emperor. Three years later when the Archbishop of Canterbury William Warham died, Henry VIII turned to Cranmer and asked him to become his new archbishop. But

---

18. Bromiley described the Cambridge years as "the most peaceful and in many ways perhaps the happiest of Cranmer's life. He was not troubled by ambitions for wealth, power or status. He had a work of reading and teaching which was wholly congenial and he had attained a position of no little importance in his own sphere. He had no financial worries, in contrast to his latter years as archbishop, when his larger income was more than absorbed by his vastly swollen expenditures. No wonder he looked back to those days with regret." Bromiley, *Thomas Cranmer*, 8.

by that time Cranmer had done two things that should have disqualified him for the office.

While on the continent serving as Henry's ambassador he had become a believer in the Reformation doctrine of justification by faith alone and, convinced that the medieval ban on clerical marriage was not biblical, he had married the niece of the wife of the Lutheran reformer Andreas Osiander. Consequently his appointment to the Archbishopric was to say the least "an unpleasant shock."[19] Although his opponents charged him with making an agreement with Henry VIII—"give me the archbishopric of Canterbury and I will give you license to live in adultery,"[20]—there is little doubt that Cranmer did not want the job. He later said "there was never a man that came more unwillingly to a bishopric than I did to that."[21] There is no reason to doubt his testimony. It is thus not surprising that he waited almost two months after having been informed of his appointment before returning home. His reluctance is understandable in view of the challenges the new Archbishop faced as he was thrown into the center of a revolution and he would be confronted with choices that would again and again challenge his moral scruples. He accepted the appointment because of his loyalty to his monarch, and the corollary belief that Henry was his God-appointed leader made him obedient even when it flew in the face of his other convictions. Cranmer's consecration took place on March 30, 1533, and he was immediately caught up in the events of the first stage of the English Reformation. His first task was to annul Henry's marriage to Catherine of Aragon and to recognize Henry's secret marriage to Anne Boleyn. Cranmer clearly had no difficulty with this because he truly believed that Henry's first marriage was invalid, besides which he thought very highly of Anne. He also did not find it difficult to support the parliamentary legislation that declared the King to be the Supreme Head of the Church in England and systematically eliminated papal authority in England, because he was convinced that the papal authority was not in accord with biblical teaching. He considered papal power in England to be an usurpation and an infringement on the King's rightful authority.

Although Cranmer's theology was considerably more evangelical than that of his monarch, he was prepared "to bide his time and wait on God's

19. MacCulluch, *Cranmer*, 77.
20. Ridley, *Thomas Cranmer*, 51.
21. Cranmer, *Works*, II, ed. Cox, 216.

providence."[22] During the 1530s, working together with the King's chief minister, Thomas Cromwell, he was able to further the evangelical cause. The central motive for Cranmer's behavior throughout Henry's reign was the preservation and furtherance of Reformation theology in England, and in that he had a surprising degree of success. In that effort, Cranmer did not hesitate to disagree with the King, and even to criticize his theology as well as his grammar, as he did in reacting to Henry VIII's comments on the so-called Bishops' Book in 1537. However, it was not easy to serve as Henry VIII's Archbishop because in doing so Cranmer inevitably became associated with the King's atrocities. Henry was not a gentle person and Cranmer found himself faced with having to accept things which violated his moral scruples.

Cranmer was first confronted with the execution of his fellow humanists, John Fisher and Thomas More. Although he tried to save their lives by advocating that they be offered a form of the oath of succession that would not compromise their consciences, he was unsuccessful. Probably the greatest blow to Cranmer was when the King turned against Anne Boleyn who had done so much to further the evangelical cause. It is to his great credit that he alone among those in high position—and that included Anne's father—came to her defense. When everyone was abandoning Anne, Cranmer courageously wrote the King extolling her virtues. In the end, he bowed to the inevitable when evidence of her guilt was presented to him. Nevertheless, he still sent the letter and he was deeply grieved by her execution. When he was informed of it, he commented: "She who had been queen of England on earth will today become a queen in heaven,"[23] and then he broke down in tears.

Cromwell's disgrace and execution was another blow to Cranmer. Once again he wrote the King a letter praising Cromwell and expressing his concern that the King was losing a brilliant advisor. In the letter he stated, "I loved him as my friend, for so I took him to be."[24] There seems little doubt that losing the man who played such an important role in leading England in the direction of a Protestant reformation was a terrible blow to the Arch-

22. Bernard, *The King's Reformation*, 605. Bernard argues that Henry was responsible for whatever theological changes occurred in his reign and that Cranmer was involved in furthering "the king's reformation . . . rather than the protestant reformation." However, clearly Cranmer and Henry had different ideas about what constituted a true biblical reform of the church.

23. PRO, S.P.70/7/659 ff. 7v–8r cited in MacCulloch, *Cranmer*, 159.

24. Cranmer, *Works*, II, ed. Cox, 401.

bishop. But, after writing the letter, he again accepted what he could not change and he joined with the other Lords in voting through Cromwell's attainder, which resulted in his friend's execution.

One of the major achievements of Cromwell and Cranmer was the 1538 Injunction that ordered an English Bible be placed in every parish church in the realm.[25] In the following year, however, the direction of the government's religious policy moved in a radically conservative direction with the passage of the Act of Six Articles. Cranmer now found himself in an especially difficult position. Other evangelicals resigned their sees or left the country, but although he urged others to flee, Cranmer felt obligated to remain and to continue the struggle to save what he could of the progress that had been achieved. Cranmer's dilemma is revealed in a statement he made to a Lutheran friend whom he urged to flee England before he was forced to give assent to the Six Articles. Cranmer commented: "Happy man that you are. You can escape. Would that I were at liberty to do the same; truly my see would not hold me back. You must escape before the island may be cut off, unless you are willing to sign the decree, as I have done."[26] Although Cranmer said he signed it out of fear, one suspects that he did it because he knew that was the only way he could remain in England and continue the struggle to save what he could of the progress that had been made in the direction of a truly Protestant church in England.

During the next seven years Cranmer was under constant attack and would very likely have suffered the fate of Anne and Cromwell if the King had not protected him. During the last years of Henry's reign three efforts were made to destroy Cranmer. First he was accused by his own prebendaries, second he was attacked in Parliament, and finally he was summoned by fellow members of the Council who intended to commit him to the tower. In each case he survived because of the King's support. At the same time, he continued the fight to preserve the availability of an English Bible to the general population and to prevent the total rejection of the Protestant doctrine of justification. Although some limitations were imposed on Scripture reading and a new statement of doctrine called the King's Book

---

25. Cranmer was overjoyed when Henry VIII approved an English Bible and he expressed his delight in a letter to Cromwell in which he exclaimed that "you have shown me more pleasure herein, than if you had given me a thousand pounds." In addition he commented that Cromwell's contribution to the approval of an English Bible "shall so much redound to your honour that, besides God's reward you shall obtain perpetual memory for the same within this realm." MacCulloch, *Cranmer*, 197.

26. MacCulloch, *Cranmer*, 251.

was considerably more Catholic in its theology than the earlier Bishops' Book, the English Bible continued to be available. Cranmer also wrote the first English litany for the Church of England, and he prepared the homilies which would be used in Edward's reign. His final service to Henry VIII came at the old King's death when Cranmer was called to his bedside. Mac-Culloch describes the scene as follows:

> Then the Archbishop, exhorting him to put his trust in Christ, and to call upon his mercy, desired him, though he could not speak, yet to give some token with his eyes or with his hand, that he trusted in the Lord. Then the king, holding him with his hand did wring his hand as hard as he could. Quietly playing out his calling as royal chaplain, Cranmer had won a final victory in his years of argument with the king on justification. No last rites for Henry, no extreme unction; just an evangelical statement of faith in the grip of his hand.[27]

When Henry VIII died on January 28, 1547, Cranmer was fifty-seven years old. After all those years of frustration and waiting, he finally had his opportunity to lead the way to what he considered a true Reformation of the English church. With the boy King Edward VI on the throne and his uncle the Duke of Somerset as Lord Protector, Cranmer now had an opportunity to introduce the type of changes he felt were necessary to build a church in England which conformed to biblical teaching. However, it was only a brief window of opportunity as Edward died on July 6, 1553, and was succeeded by his Roman Catholic sister, Mary. Furthermore, even during Edward's brief reign, Cranmer faced serious opposition and there were even divisions among those who were supporters of the Protestant Reformation. Cranmer began Edward's reign by urging the new King to be "a second Josiah," and he proceeded in the years that followed to carry out what amounted to a religious revolution. But it was done cautiously and with great sensitivity to the beliefs of those who were not yet ready for a more radical step. However, as he stated in a letter to Calvin, he remained committed to a thorough biblically-based reform of the English church.[28]

He never relented in that effort, and his well-known accomplishments during the brief period when he had a relatively free hand were by any

---

27. MacCulloch, *Cranmer*, 360.

28. "We will reform the English church to the utmost of our ability and give our labour that both its doctrines and laws will be improved after the model of Holy Scripture" MacCulloch, *Cranmer*, 520.

standard quite remarkable. One is amazed that a busy Archbishop who was nearing the age when many people are thinking of retirement achieved so much in such a short period of time. Those were also certainly not trouble-free years as the government was faced with a rebellion against the new Prayer Book, resistance from conservative prelates, and pressure from more radical Protestants to make more changes.[29] His old nemesis Stephen Gardiner, the Bishop of Winchester, challenged Cranmer's first significant move in the direction of Protestant theology with good legal arguments that Cranmer found difficult to refute. When at the end of July 1547 a series of royal injunctions were issued that ordered clergy to read Cranmer's Homilies which taught the Protestant doctrine of justification by faith, Gardiner protested that this order was in violation of statute law which forbade teaching contrary to the King's Book. Gardiner was, in fact, right and it was only when the first parliament of Edward's reign repealed the statute, that Cranmer's first cautious steps in the direction of a truly Protestant reformation became technically legal.[30]

Cranmer also witnessed the fall and eventual execution of the Duke of Somerset who had worked with him in the initial stages of the Edwardian Reformation. Once again Cranmer came to the defense of a colleague and it seems that this helped to create a breach between the Archbishop and the new head of the King's government, John Dudley, the Duke of Northumberland. Cranmer's relationship with the Duke was clearly tense and when in a letter to Queen Mary he stated that Northumberland's "heart was not toward me (seeking long time my destruction)."[31] Cranmer was probably not exaggerating. However, even as Cranmer was becoming more and more estranged from Northumberland, he still managed to produce the 1552 Prayer Book, the Forty-Two Articles, and a major revision of the canon law. He also faced new disappointments as he failed in his effort to bring about an ecumenical council of Protestants in England and his canon law revision was not adopted by Parliament. Finally, he was confronted

29. Peter Martyr commented: "The perverseness of the bishops is incredible. They oppose us with all their might. But the weight of hostility only enhances the pertinacity of the archbishop" Cranmer, *Works,* II, ed. Cox, 486.

30. For a more thorough discussion of the confrontation between Gardiner and Cranmer see Heinze, *Proclamations,* 205ff.

31. Cranmer, *Works,* II, ed. Cox, 444. "By the end of 1551 the Archbishop had fallen from favor. Between 18 April, 1552, and 16 June, 1553, Cranmer was present at only 28 out of a possible 218 meetings of the Privy Council" Paul Ayris, the relationship between the crown and the Archbishopric." Ayris and Selwyn, *Thomas Cranmer,* 145.

with new opposition by more radical Protestants like John Hooper who attacked Cranmer's Ordinal for mentioning the saints in the oath of supremacy and retaining the vestments in the rite of consecration. Cranmer found the outspoken Scotsman, John Knox, who had become a favorite of the Duke of Northumberland, especially irritating when Knox attacked the provision for kneeling at communion in the 1552 Prayer Book. Cranmer reacted in a long letter to the Council in which he expressed his anger and frustration with those who were always seeking more radical changes. He wrote: "I know your lordships' wisdom be such that I trust ye will not be moved with these glorious [vainglorious] and unquiet spirits, which can like nothing but that is after their own fancy and cease not to make trouble and disquietness when things be most quiet and in good order."[32] Nevertheless, the Council added the so-called Black Rubric to the 1552 Prayer Book, explaining that kneeling at communion did not involve adoration of the host despite Cranmer's objections.[33]

Cranmer's troubles at the end of Edward's reign were infinitesimal compared to what awaited him as Queen Mary ascended the throne. It seems ironic that the man who was least equipped in his personal makeup to be a martyr was the one who was asked to pay the ultimate price for his commitment to the gospel. Both Luther and Calvin would have made outstanding martyrs, but Cranmer's ability to see both sides of the argument, his readiness to accept compromise solutions, and his inborn timidity made it difficult for him to stand firm under the sufferings he experienced at the end of his life. We often tend to focus on the physical suffering and the brainwashing that Cranmer endured during his imprisonment, and neglect to consider the mental and spiritual anguish he must have suffered as he saw all that he had labored to achieve destroyed by Mary. He was sixty-four years old when Mary ascended the throne and it is to his great credit that he stayed to fight for the things he believed even though he must have known that he had little chance of preserving them. He could have fled to the continent as he advised others to do, but he stayed and did not remain silent, when the wisest course of action would have been not to draw attention to oneself. In fact, early in the reign he offered to defend: "Not only the

32. Ayris and Selwyn, *Thomas Cranmer*, 145.

33. It was called the Black Rubric because having been added after the book was already printed it was printed in black rather than the conventional red in which the other rubrics were printed. See the discussion in MacCulloch, *Cranmer*, 526ff. who maintains that the insertion of the Black Rubric was not a defeat for Cranmer's position on the Eucharist.

common prayers of the churches, ministration of the sacraments, and other rites and ceremonies, but also that all the doctrine and religion, by our said sovereign Lord King Edward VI is more pure and according to God's word, than any that hath been used in England these thousand years."[34]

Those were not the words of a coward, and they sealed his fate. His declaration was made public on September 8th and six days later he was in prison. Cranmer spent almost two and a half years in prison, and during that time he was subjected to the most intense pressure and clever brainwashing to get him to recant. Cranmer's trials, both formal and mental, as well as the specifics of his six recantations need not be retold for the purposes of this study.[35] One can, however, appreciate somewhat the enormous distress Cranmer must have experienced during those long years in prison, often in total isolation, as he learned about the systematic destruction of all he had achieved, saw his friends brutally murdered, and had the contradictions in his own thinking exposed. The fact that he eventually broke and signed one recantation after another should not surprise us. Rather, the amazing thing is that before his death he renounced those recantations and died courageously. The enduring picture of Cranmer which is recorded in the pages of Fox is that of the old Archbishop at the stake thrusting the hand that signed the recantations into the fire and crying with a loud voice "this hand hath offended." He then died with the words of Stephen on his lips "Lord Jesus receive my spirit. . . . I see the heavens open and Jesus standing at the right hand of God."[36]

The critical question we need now to address is how did Cranmer manage to stand up to all the challenges he faced and continue to carry on his important work? Where did he find the strength to endure the long years of disappointment and delay in Henry VIII's reign? How did he manage as he witnessed Henry's brutal treatment of people he admired and who had worked with him for the reform of the church? Where did he find the patience to keep waiting and working when he experienced one setback after another and saw many of his earlier achievements undermined by the conservative reaction at the end of Henry's reign? How did he survive

34. Cranmer, *Works,* II, ed. Cox, 428–29.

35. MacCulloch, *Cranmer,* 554ff. for an account of Cranmer's trials and his recantations. For an account with a slightly different emphasis, see Heinze, "I Pray God to Grant that I may Endure to the Ends: A New Look at the Martyrdom of Thomas Cranmer," in Ayris and Selwyn, *Thomas Cranmer,* 261ff.

36. Townsend and Cattley, *Acts and Monuments of John Foxe,* 90; MacCulloch, *Cranmer,* 603–4.

constant opposition and resistance to what he believed was the God ordained reform that he was called to bring to the Church of England? How
did he cope with the disappointment he must have felt in Edward's reign
when divisions occurred in the ranks of those committed to the theology
of the Reformation and when the revision of canon law to which he had
devoted so much time and effort failed to be enacted? Finally, how did he
manage to endure during Mary's reign when it seemed that everything he
had achieved in his life and that he had worked for so long and hard would
be destroyed?

As pointed out earlier, Cranmer was a very private person so he sel-
dom if ever revealed in his writings how he managed to endure, but we
can find hints by looking at what he wrote to strengthen and help others in
their Christian walk. First and foremost Cranmer inevitably advised others to turn to the Word of God for strength and guidance in the midst
of trouble. In the well-known Preface to the Great Bible of 1540 Cranmer
advised those who were facing trouble and worldly dangers to turn to the
Scriptures. He pointed out that those who have an easy, trouble free life did
not need the same kind of help that those confronted with constant challenges needed. He wrote:

> So much the more it is behoveful for thee to have defense of scrip-
> tures, how much thou are the more distressed in worldly dangers.
> . . . Thou art in the midst of the sea of worldly wickedness, and
> therefore thou needest the more of ghostly succor and comfort!
> . . . Thou that standest in the forefront of the host, and nighest to
> thine enemies, must needs take now and then many strokes, and
> be grievously wounded, and therefore thou has more need to have
> thy remedies and medicines at hand. . . . Briefly, so divers and so
> manifold occasions of cares, tribulations, and temptations beset
> thee and besiege thee round about. Where canst thou have armor
> or fortress against thine assaults? Where canst thou have salves for
> thy sores, but of Holy Scripture?[37]

One suspects Cranmer was speaking out of his own experience when
he wrote those words, and it would not be surprising that again and again,
he must have found the strength to continue his struggle in the scriptures
whose availability in English was due in large part to his efforts. His homily on the Reading of Holy Scripture equally stressed the importance of

---

37. Cranmer, *Works,* II, ed. Cox, 119–20. Cranmer was quoting from a sermon of
John Chrysostom.

Scripture for providing Christians with the true doctrine and the strength to endure. In that sermon he stated: "Unto a Christian Man, there can be nothing either more necessary, or profitable than the knowledge of Holy Scripture, forasmuch as in it is contained God's true word, setting forth his glory, and also man's duty. And there is no truth nor doctrine, necessary for our justification, and everlasting salvation, but that is, or may be, drawn out of that fountain and well of truth. Therefore, as many as may be desirous to enter into the right, and perfect way unto God, must apply their minds to know Holy Scripture."[38]

Secondly, there is no doubt that Cranmer was a man of prayer. He who wrote so many prayers for others, many of which are still used today, must have spent many hours on his knees before his Lord asking for strength. We could turn to many of Cranmer's prayers to illustrate how he taught others to pray for strength in the midst of challenges and adversities, but it is especially revealing to turn to the first English prayers that he wrote in 1544. At that time he was under great personal danger and he was witnessing many of his previous reform efforts being undermined. In his litany he included the following prayer:

> Oh God, merciful father, that despisest not the sighing of a contrite heart, or the desire of such as be sorrowful, mercifully assist our prayers, that we make before thee in all our troubles and adversities, when so ever they oppress us. And graciously hear us, that those evils, which the craft and subtlety of the devil or man worketh against us, be brought to naught, and by the providence of thy goodness they may be dispersed; that we, thy servants, being hurt by no persecution, may evermore give thanks unto thee in thy holy church, though Jesu Christ our lord.[39]

A third source of Cranmer's strength that enabled him to continue in the face of his own personal failures was the gospel that he worked so hard to incorporate into the teaching of the Church of England. Cranmer was far from a perfect servant of Christ and he knew it. Again and again he made compromises that must have bothered his conscience, and he confessed several times that it was his lack of courage that caused him to act in a way that in hindsight he could not admire. He must have often felt that he

---

38. "A fruitful exhortation to the Reading of Holy Scripture," *Homilies*, 4.

39. *The First and Second Prayer Books of Edward VI*, 234. Although the prayer was first included in the 1544 litany, that litany was included in both Edwardian prayer books largely unaltered and is also in the 1662 Prayer Book.

had not served his Lord as well as he felt called to do, and he must have felt many times that he had let others down and failed to stand as strongly as he should have. It is at those times when the gospel must have become especially meaningful to him. Cranmer wrote the following words in his *Homily of Faith*:

> and that although we through infirmity, or temptation of our ghostly enemy, do fall from him [God] by sin, yet if we return again unto him by true repentance, that he will forgive and forget our offences for his Son's sake, our Saviour Jesus Christ, and will make us inheritors with him of his everlasting kingdom; and that in the meantime, until that kingdom come, he will be our protector and defender, in all perils and dangers, whatsoever do chance; and that though sometime he doth send us sharp adversity, ye that evermore he will be a loving father unto us, correcting us for our sin, but not withdrawing his mercy finally from us, if we trust in him, and commit ourselves wholly to him, hang only upon him, and call upon him, ready to obey and serve him.[40]

That confidence in the Lord's mercy in Jesus Christ carried him through to the end, and it is reflected in the prayer he wrote as he prepared to die, which he prayed at St. Mary's church before his final statement retracting his recantations:

> I who have offended both heaven and earth and more grievously than any tongue can express whither then may I go, or whither should I fly for succor? To heaven I may be ashamed to lift up mine eyes, and in earth I find no refuge or succor. What shall I then do? Shall I despair? God forbid. Oh good God, thou art merciful and refuseth none that cometh unto thee for succor. To thee therefore do I run. To Thee do I humble myself; saying O Lord God, my sins be great yet have mercy upon me for thy great mercy.[41]

A final and vital element in Cranmer's ability to endure, in the face of so many challenges and disappointments, was that he continued to have confidence that it is *God* who decides what will happen in his church and not us. It is also God and not our personal strength that will provide for us as we seek to serve him in our inadequate and sometimes even misguided way. In 1549, when the German church was experiencing particular trials

40. Cranmer, *Works*, II, ed. Cox, 135.
41. *Works of Thomas Cranmer*, ed. Duffield, 334.

as the result of the defeat of the Lutheran princes by the Catholic emperor, Cranmer wrote to Philip Melanchthon:

> We are experiencing, most learned Melanchthon, the truth of all that our Lord Jesus Christ has foretold respecting the trials of his church. "But God is faithful, who will not suffer his people to be tempted above that they are able, but will also with the temptation make a way to escape, that we may be able to bear it." For though from his hatred to the Son of God the devil exercises a horrible tyranny over the members of Christ, yet God has promised that his church shall never perish; nay, of these last times he expressly declares, "to hoar hairs will I carry her; I will bear, I will deliver her."[42]

Cranmer's confidence in God's provision was tested to the utmost in the last years of his life, and he came very close to dying in disgrace rather than as a courageous martyr. However, in the end he found the strength he needed in the final hours of his earthly life. He was aware that he could only survive in the strength of God as he faced those final trials. In what was probably the last letter he ever wrote, he confided to his good friend Peter Martyr how God upheld him in his struggles. At a time when he knew that his strength was gone and he may have feared that he was about to give in to his tormentor's efforts to get him to recant he wrote the following words to Peter:

> God never shines forth more brightly, and pours out the beams of his mercy and consolation, or of strength and firmness of spirit, more clearly or impressively upon the minds of his people, than when they are under the most extreme pain and distress, both of mind and body, that he may then more especially shew himself to be the God of his people, when he seems to have altogether forsaken them; then raising them up when they think he is bringing them down, and laying them low; then glorifying them, when he is thought to be confounding them; then quickening them, when he is thought to be destroying them; so that we may say with Paul, "when I am weak, then am I strong; and if I must needs glory, I will glory in my infirmities, in prisons, in revilings, in distresses, in persecutions, in sufferings for Christ." I pray God to grant that I may endure to the end.[43]

42. Cranmer, *Works*, II, ed. Cox, 426.

43. Ibid., 457–58.

Cranmer could easily identify with the Apostle Paul's words "when I'm weak then I'm strong" because in his many struggles this "timid man struggling to be brave" recognized his own weakness and therefore had to rely on the God he trusted and sought to serve for strength in order to endure. Although his accomplishments were massive, he would have been the first to insist that none of it was accomplished in his own strength. Over half a century ago G. R. Bromiley commended Cranmer's accomplishments, while at the same time recognizing the difficulties he faced in achieving his goals. One suspects that Dr. Toon would echo Bromiley's assessment of Thomas Cranmer's greatness as well as his contributions to the Anglican Way:

> The real greatness of Cranmer emerges only when we either share his fundamental positions or at least enter into the thinking and motives which inspired him and the situations which he confronted. It is then that we appreciate the slow but steady progress to evangelical truth of the one who had the caution and integrity of a genuine scholar. It is then that we understand something of the constructive policy of reform and can admire the skill and tenacity with which it was carried through in circumstances which he could never directly control and which were seldom entirely favorable. . . . In spite of the changes and chances of centuries, in its underlying aspects, in its more basic and enduring characteristics the Church of England still bears plainly the imprint of the work and witness of Thomas Cranmer. For those who love that Church, its open Bible, its dignified but pure and scriptural worship, its profession of reformed and evangelical truth there can be no more eloquent or comprehensive tribute.[44]

---

44. Bromiley, *Thomas Cranmer*, 120–21.

3

Worship, the Moral Life, and Political Community: The Cranmerian Prayer Book Legacy

JOAN LOCKWOOD O'DONOVAN

This essay presents the thematic core of a larger project, which may be described as a critical and constructive retrieval of the English Reformation theology of church establishment.[1] As the relationship of church and state is central and not peripheral to this theology, it has of its very nature a moral, social, and political orientation. It has also a public orientation, its historical sources being chiefly public documents from the Tudor period (i.e., from the reigns of Henry VIII, Edward VI, and Elizabeth I). These include the body of Tudor church legislation erected on the Henrician statutes, the officially licensed or authorized vernacular Bibles preceding the King James Version, three editions of the Book of Common Prayer with the accompanying or incorporated Ordinals, and finally, the Forty-Two and Thirty-Nine Articles and the Books of Homilies issued under King Edward and Queen Elizabeth. These public documents provided the theoretical

---

1. As well as anticipating a fuller treatment of its themes, it also builds on past discussions: most notably, the essays "A Reformation Ethics: Proclamation and Jurisdiction as Determinants of Moral Agency and Action," and "The Church's Worship and the Moral Life: An Anglican Contribution to Trinitarian Ethic."

foundations and guiding framework for an English ecclesial, moral, and political tradition.

Of these documents, the theologically most influential in the English church, after the printed Bibles, have been the Tudor editions of the prayer book. As many readers will know, the Edwardian 1552 edition, with some key insertions from the earlier 1549 edition, comprised the Elizabethan edition of 1559, and subsequently, the bulk of the 1662 Book of Common Prayer, which remained for more than three centuries the only legally prescribed order of worship (i.e., prescribed by parliamentary act) for the English national church on ordinary, festive, and state occasions. Exported around the world through British colonial and missionary enterprises, the 1662 Book of Common Prayer has supplied the historical foundations of liturgical development in most other Anglican churches in the world today.

It is historically ironic, then, that the legal establishment presupposed by the 1662 prayer book is the one feature of the Church of England that has unequivocally divided her over generations from practically all of her "daughter churches," whether they were disestablished over time, or never were established. This dimension of their inheritance has necessarily been ignored, or at least sidelined, in order to accommodate the political and legal, social and cultural realities in which they had been founded, or subsequently found themselves. Such accommodation, however necessary or desirable in each case, has not left entirely intact the moral and political vision of the English prayer book tradition. It is this theological vision that I wish to sketch, as I am convinced that it remains an instructive and challenging legacy for Anglican and other Christian churches.

I must hasten to add the further historical irony that the whole vision of the English prayer book tradition is no longer intact in the Church of England either. The last fifty years of large-scale liturgical revision has resulted in, on the one hand, a continuing proliferation of liturgies, and on the other, a steady trend toward simpler ecumenical and Catholic forms that underplay certain controlling principles and emphases of the historic prayer books. The demise in parish churches of traditional Sunday services of Matins and Evensong, together with a more Catholic handling of the weekly "parish Eucharist" has led, broadly speaking, to the loss of lengthy and coherent Scripture readings and of preaching which takes seriously the task of Scriptural exposition. These liturgical reforms have entailed a distancing from core Reformation themes, and as well, the sacrifice of liturgical solemnity and beauty for popular accessibility. Within the more self-consciously evangelical constituency, which sustains a focus on Scripture reading and exposition, worship has consistently veered in a populist, youth-oriented, informal, and non-liturgical direction.

Running parallel with these liturgical trends in the Church of England, there has been a progressive weakening and dismantling of other aspects of historic church establishment: of the national scope and public prominence of the church's parochial and non-parochial ministries, and of the interconnections of ecclesial and civil government. While English church-state relations are currently in some constitutional flux, it would appear that an increasingly pluralistic religious establishment is taking shape, involving Christian and non-Christian communities, which the civil authorities will attempt to manage more aggressively than previously, through multilateral consultative and co-operative arrangements or "partnerships."[2]

It is worthy of note that not all religious and non-religious constituencies on English soil are persuaded that their spiritual and practical interests will be best served by trading the constitutional umbrella and distinctive public presence of traditional church establishment for a government-orchestrated pluralism of individual and communal religious rights. Some distrust the ethos of the emerging establishment as being excessively managerial, legalistic, and juridical. They may justifiably fear the specter of religious groups and their members conducting themselves as self-protecting proprietors, jealous of their own powers of self-disposal, as centers of competitive demand for public resources (symbolic and material), enmeshed

---

2. At the same time as the interconnections of civil and ecclesiastical government are being loosened by such ongoing developments as the British Parliament's House of Lord's reform, which may see the removal of some or all of the twenty-six senior bishops who traditionally sit in the upper chamber, initiatives have proliferated across government departments to launch multilateral relations with diverse "faith communities" in the provision of public religious ministries and charitable services. These multilateral relations, in which the Church of England is one among equals, are increasingly superseding the longstanding bilateral relations in which she has functioned since the nineteenth century as *primus inter pares*—as broker and gatekeeper, enabling other Christian denominations and religious communities to access state resources in developing and sustaining their public ministries. Chaplaincies in public institutions (more notably in prisons and hospitals than in the more conservative armed forces) exemplify the recent shift from statutory and administrative frameworks that recognize the primacy of the Church of England, while accommodating other denominations and groups, to a reforming agenda of implementing religious diversity and equality. The reforming agenda has proceeded through the formation of "multi-faith" advisory and administrative bodies and operational guidelines that are not "faith-specific," but diversity-inclusive. For an overview of these developments, see Rivers, *The Law of Organized Religions*, chs. 7, 9, 10.

in externally regulated relationships with one another, in which each is continually assessing another's claims and another's compliance with the rules, and always vigilant that government adjudication of religious rights is sufficiently uniform and egalitarian.

Such a legalistic, juridical, and managerial ethos is one of which we all have had experience, as it is threatening to permeate every social and institutional sphere and enterprise across our egalitarian rights societies. It is increasingly recognized (but to little practical effect!) that an oppressive surveillance of rights provision and protection, combined with the pervasive threat of litigation, is inflating the public and private regulation of social institutions, organizations and agencies, with the imposition of inappropriate and counter-productive standards of rationality, efficiency, probity, and justice. Invasive regulation is today depriving many who labor in diverse fields of work, care, and professional endeavor of their proper freedom of judgment and the exercise of their skills and wisdom as experienced practitioners.

Theologically considered, these destructive social and political trends are the contemporary form of sinful human striving after justification by works of the law, and, concomitantly, both cause and symptom of our diminished participation in the real spiritual and material goods of human community. As we struggle with the current ethos, it is salutary to retrieve from the Cranmerian prayer book legacy an understanding of human moral agency, action, and community as primarily evangelical or proclamatory, conformed to the church's practice of worship, and only secondarily and peripherally as juridical, conformed to the practice of secular jurisdiction. This I now hope to do in the space available.

The Dialectic of Proclamation and Jurisdiction

Let me begin by situating the moral and political vision of the Cranmerian prayer books within the broader theological approach to moral community characterizing the mainstream of English reformers.[3] This approach envisions the moral life of persons-in-society as controlled by two universal authorities and practices: on the one hand, the authority of God's saving word of judgment given in Jesus Christ, which is directly constitutive of the

3. In the reforming mainstream I would include such Henrician and Elizabethan theologians and lawyers as William Tyndale, Christopher St. German, Thomas Cranmer, Thomas Cromwell, Richard Sampson, Edward Fox, Thomas Starkey, William Marshall, John Rogers, Hugh Latimer, Nicholas Ridley, John Ponet, John Jewel, and John Whitgift.

church's practice of proclamation; on the other, the authority of the human practice of coercive jurisdiction operating under God's word of judgment. These two authorities and practices determine human moral agency and action as they belong to the order of God's good creation in its twofold eschatological and historical reality: as restored and awaiting its fulfillment through Christ's conquest of sin and death on the cross, and as still struggling under the wages of sin and subject to the law's condemnation. While the English reformers insisted on a theoretical and institutional separation of these different, even antithetical, communal practices, they also recognized their interdependence in this eschatological age in which the Old Adam is being overtaken by the New.

For the English reformers, as for their continental mentors, it is in the church's practice of proclamation that human moral agency and action is renewed and human goods decisively appropriated, where God's judgments are heard and received by the community. The Reformers conceive renewed moral agency and action as human judgment between good and evil conforming to God's own judgments, and coming to fruition in human action. The first and determinative human judgment, which forms the ground and possibility of all others, is the individual and communal judgment of faith, in which sinful human beings accept the Father's judgment of condemnation and reconciliation directed toward themselves in the death and resurrection of his Son, Jesus Christ. The Father's judgment of condemnation and reconciliation is, at one and the same time, his condemnation (invalidation) of the history of sinful human judgment and action, his vindication (validation) of faithful human judgment and action within the order of his good creation, and his promise of future fulfillment of all that he has vindicated in raising and exalting Jesus Christ. The individual and communal act of faith, then, is a complex act of repentance, belief, and hope.

The continental and English reformers emphatically present the act of faith as originating not within sinful human subjectivity, but within the divine subjectivity of the Holy Spirit, who, as the Spirit of the risen and ascended Christ, incorporates believers into Christ's resurrection life and makes available to them the spiritual benefits of their redemption. As the Spirit communicates Christ's benefits in a pre-eminent way in the practice of worship, of word and sacrament, so it is within this regular communal practice that faith is generated, nourished, strengthened, and purified. Indeed, the reformers regard worship as the faithful people's ongoing common reception of the Father's reconciling judgment in Jesus Christ, and the central communicative act of their faith. On this account, they may be said to regard faith as a gift of the Holy Spirit to the assembled church before it is a gift to its individual members; and, moreover, to regard common worship as the first practical obedience of faith, and as paradigmatic for all obedience.[4]

The reformers' conviction that the renewal of human moral freedom springs from the church's practice of gospel proclamation, rather than from juridical practice, was the moral correlate to their soteriological conviction that sinful human beings are justified solely by God's grace in Christ and not by their works. As judgment over the faithful belongs exclusively to God in Christ who is both judge and judged, so the primary response of the faithful to God's judgment in Christ is one of evangelical proclamation—of joyful, humble, and adoring worship—rather than one of public judgment, whether in the civil or ecclesiastical realms. In one theological move the reformers repudiated the medieval Roman conception of the church as a priestly hierarchy of proclamation wedded to jurisdiction, and the medieval discipline of sacramental penance in which priests, besides "retaining or remitting" the guilt of sins, judged confessing sinners as to their degrees of sin and guilt, and assigned earthly punishments (penances).[5]

Correspondingly, the mainstream of English Reformers, following Luther, reinterpreted the apostolic authority of the ordained ministry as essentially proclamatory and non-jurisdictional: they had authority to preach and teach God's word, to intercede on behalf of the gathered church, to give pastoral counsel, exhortation, and consolation to those within their care; and they reinforced this interpretation by assigning jurisdiction over

4. My choice of terms here expresses my debt to Bernd Wannenwetsch's rich exploration of the church's common worship as the "grammar of Christian life" and the "first instance" of her corporate obedience to God's rule, in *Gottesdienst als Lebensform—Ethik für Christenbürger,* translated by Kohl, *Political Worship: Ethics for Christian Citizens.*

5. Medieval thought inherited from the patristic church a conception of the bishop's unified sacramental and jurisdictional powers exercised in the discipline of public penance. The medieval bishop's exercise of the church's "power of the keys" retained the intimate relationship between judgment in the sphere of conscience (*iurisdictio in foro interiori* to use a late medieval term) and jurisdiction in the church's external polity (*iurisdictio in foro exteriori*) despite tendencies toward their separation (e.g., the growth of private sacramental penance on the one hand, and of papal jurisdictional supremacy on the other). In so far as medieval penitential theology and especially the theory of papal indulgences placed human juridical acts at the core of the church's mediation of salvation in Christ, the evangelical reformers were moved to jettison both *fora* of priestly jurisdiction together.

external church polity to the lay magistrate and his ecclesiastical representatives.[6] The predominant Anglican view was that episcopal jurisdiction in the church's external polity derived from the royal "plenitude" and had no independent christological basis; so that when the bishops issued binding public judgments in whatever ecclesiastical sphere (doctrinal, liturgical, administrative, disciplinary), they did so as the monarch's ministers.[7]

Let us now turn to the Cranmerian prayer books, to explore their understanding of the paradigmatic role of public worship in determining moral agency and action as evangelical proclamation. But first, a very brief word must be offered on their content, and on Thomas Cranmer's contribution to their production.[8]

6. This reinterpretation was, of course, anticipated by such late-medieval reforming theologians as Marsiglio of Padua and John Wyclif, whose theological strategy was to reinterpret the clerical exercise of judgment in both the interior and exterior *fora* as non-jurisdictional; so that the priestly power of "binding and loosing" became the power of discerning and declaring to the church God's prior work of retaining or remitting guilt, and episcopal authority became the superior authority of teaching and pastoral oversight. In respect of the penitential discipline, however, Marsiglio's reinterpretation faltered over the doctrines of purgatory and substitutionary satisfactions: it took Wyclif and his Protestant successors to jettison the papal economy of grace and merit in which a juridical logic still inhered. The early English reformers, as much as their continental colleagues, prosecuted a relentless assault on the juridical logic of sacramental penance, from their novel theological standpoint of justification through faith alone. Some of them, like William Tyndale and Thomas Cranmer, perceived the crucial link between sacramental and political jurisdiction in the papal church, but they were unable to persuade King Henry VIII, who remained incorrigibly attached to the old practices and a theology of "works righteousness."

7. This reforming view was only consistently challenged in the 1570s by the rise of Calvinist ecclesiology. Archbishop Cranmer's attempt in 1540 to reconcile this position with the New Testament record of the apostolic church reflected the Eusebian legacy of Marsiglio and Wyclif that was, undoubtedly, widely shared. He argued that the apostolic church, far from providing the foundation for episcopal jurisdiction, was constrained by necessity to function in a jurisdictional vacuum. In the absence of a divinely ordained Christian ruler with authority to appoint ministers and to correct vice, church appointments and discipline could only proceed by "the consent of the Christian multitude among themselves," sometimes selecting from within their midst, at other times accepting commendations from the godly, or gratefully receiving apostolic appointments. While acknowledging the exemplary virtue of the early Christian community and its reverence for apostolic wisdom, Cranmer clearly indicated that God's plans for the governance of his church only reached fruition with the advent of Christian empire. He advanced this argument in answering questions addressed to members of a doctrinal commission. Cox, *Miscellaneous Writings*, 116–17.

8. Thomas Cranmer (1489–1556) served as Archbishop of Canterbury for twenty years, until Mary Tudor's accession to the English throne in 1553. While a Fellow of

The original and revised books of 1549 and 1552 contain all the orders of English services, including the daily offices of Morning and Evening Prayer, the Litany, the ministration of Holy Communion, public and private Baptism, Confirmation, the Solemnization of Matrimony, Visitation and Communion of the Sick, and Burial of the Dead—the ordination and consecration of deacons, priests, and bishops occupying a separate book until the 1552 revision. These new orders were variously related to their medieval English predecessors, some more closely, some more remotely. Minimally, their production involved translation, shortening, and simplification of the old Latin liturgies, to increase clerical and lay understanding and enable greater lay participation. Frequently it involved more radical overhauling of their structure and content, as in the reduction of the daily monastic and clerical offices or hours from eight to two (morning and evening). Always, it involved theological reorientation to central reformation themes. Theological reorientation, along with structural modifications, was more pronounced in the 1552 edition,[9] and it was this edition that was adopted by the Elizabethan church with few significant revisions, none of which affect the following observations and reflections.

While the production of both prayer books, naturally, involved the collaboration and scrutiny of episcopal committees, their chief architect,

---

Jesus College, Cambridge, he had helped to marshal the university behind Henry VIII's proposed divorce from Catherine of Aragon, and after his archiepiscopal appointment, arranged for the annulment of this and two of Henry's subsequent marriages. The first years of his archiepiscopate saw the establishment of royal supremacy over the English church, with considerable enlargement of the ecclesiastical jurisdiction of Canterbury. His less creditable services to the king in these years were offset by his patient efforts at theological education of Henry and of the English population, his initially fruitful attempts at *rapprochement* with the Lutherans, and his joint crusade with Thomas Cromwell for the printing and dissemination of the vernacular Bible. The accession of Edward VI in 1547 enabled Cranmer to make his lasting liturgical contribution to the English church, in the production of the 1549 and 1552 Books of Common Prayer. His final years were devoted to taking the English church in a more Reformed direction, under the influence of distinguished continental refugees. Their notable achievements were the publication of the Forty-Two Articles in 1553 (which formed the basis of the Thirty-Nine Articles promulgated under Elizabeth I in 1563/1571, to which the Church of England still loosely subscribes) and a sadly abortive attempt at canon law revision.

9. E.g., the Communion saw radical structural revision, with the dismantling of the traditional sequence of prayers comprising the "Canon" of the Mass, retained in 1549. The removal and dispersion of prayers was primarily intended to eliminate any lingering suggestion of: 1) the Eucharistic celebration as a repetition of Christ's offering, and a meritorious work performed by the priest for the church; and 2) the doctrines of transubstantiation of the host, or even of Christ's corporeal presence in the received elements.

translator, adaptor, editor, and composer was Cranmer. His contribution extended beyond the liturgical texts *per se* to the design of calendars for Bible readings, psalms, and collects. It is now well understood that his inspiration and sources were far-ranging, temporally and geographically, from patristic writings to a host of more contemporary Catholic, Lutheran, and Reformed liturgies, manuals, books of private devotions, and catechisms.[10]

Common Worship as Paradigmatic for Moral Agency and Action

Let us now look more closely at how the English liturgies display the proclamatory structure of all practical obedience: i.e., how they display renewed moral agency and action as a structured response to and communication of God's word of judgment in Jesus Christ, which is his word in its trinitarian fullness.

(1) *The Common Moral Agency of the Worshipping Church.* In their content and internal organization, the English liturgies display the pivotal ethical insight that the Holy Spirit's gift of renewed moral agency is not to the individual, but to the community of persons. From 1552 onward, the voice of the worshippers is decisively the collective "we" rather than the singular "I." They convey the expectation that perfected moral agency in the kingdom of God will be wholly common, communicative, and consensual: that there will be mutual participation in the Spirit's judgments, and mutual sharing in the knowledge, love, and freedom of the risen Christ. It is this full manifestation of reconciled community that the church's practice of worship proclaims in word and deed, in preaching and sacraments. But the liturgies do not identify the gathered faithful in this age of waiting with any institutional church, or with the entirety of earthly institutional churches; nor do they affirm that institutional practices of worship are, in and of themselves, the pure moral action of reconciled community. Rather, they affirm that renewed moral humanity is visible where the word of God is purely preached and the sacraments administered according to Christ's commandments.

---

10. An introductory history of the Anglican Prayer Book is given by Hatchett's article "Prayer Books," *The Study of Anglicanism.* Longer discussions of the 1549 and 1552 Books of Common Prayer are found in Booty, *The Book of Common Prayer 1559*; Brightman, *The English Rite*; Cuming, *The Godly Order,* and *A History of Anglican Liturgy.* Also valuable are the relevant discussions in MacCulloch, *Cranmer.*

The English liturgies display the subject of every obedient act of worship as the whole community of Christ's faithful people, to which every worshipping individual and congregation is joined in a real communion of minds and wills. This communion is the Spirit's bond of faith, hope, and love that every moral act both presupposes and strengthens. The universality of the worshipping subject is expressed in the inclusion of regular prayers for the universal church,[11] of ancient confessions of faith, and of forms and prayers drawn from a wide-spectrum of ancient and contemporary sources, Eastern and Western, Roman, Lutheran and Reformed.[12]

Furthermore, the priority of the communal moral subject is expressed in the English rite of infant baptism, which, firstly, presents the incorporation of the candidate into the community of Christ's resurrection promises as God's response to the obedient prayers and confessions of the whole gathered church present in the local congregation and in the godparents;[13]

11. Although the liturgies' explicit tendency (from 1552) is to identify the church universal with "the church militant" on earth, out of reforming reticence about communion of the living with the dead in Christ, they unequivocally extend the worshiping subject across time and space.

12. Cranmer was not only ecumenical in his contemporary liturgical borrowings but frequently retained more of the tradition than even Lutheran colleagues. For example, he preserved more of the traditional canticles (regularly chanted scriptural texts), versicles, and responses in Morning and Evening Prayer, and over seventy of the church's ancient and medieval collects (set prayers), in translated and adapted forms, for which he was largely responsible. Together with his additional twenty-four original collects, "these jewelled miniatures," to quote Diarmaid MacCulloch, "are one of the chief glories of the Anglican [and Western] liturgical tradition" and "have proved one of the most enduring vehicles of worship in the [world-wide] Anglican communion." *Cranmer*, 417.

13. The service (1559) opens with this bidding addressed by the minister to the whole congregation: "Dearly beloved, forasmuch as all men be conceived and born in sin, and that our Saviour Christ saith, None can enter into the kingdom of God except he be regenerate, and born anew of water and the Holy Ghost: I beseech you to call upon God the Father, through our Lord Jesus Christ, that of his bounteous mercy he will grant to these children that thing which by nature they cannot have, that they may be baptized with water and the Holy Ghost, and received into Christ's holy Church, and be made lively members of the same." Booty, *The Book of Common Prayer 1559*, 270. All liturgical quotations are from this edition, hereafter abbreviated *BCP*. Subsequently, the minister addresses the god-parents before they make promises for the candidate: "Well beloved friends, ye have brought these children here to be baptized; ye have prayed that our Lord Jesus Christ would vouchsafe to receive them, to lay his hands upon them, to bless them, to release them of their sins, to give them the kingdom of heaven, and everlasting life. Ye have heard also that our Lord Jesus Christ hath promised in his gospel [Mark 10:13–16] to grant all these things that ye have prayed for; which promise he for his part will surely keep and perform." *BCP*, 272–73.

and secondly, it presents the pledges of openness to Christ's promises made for the candidate by the godparents as the candidate's own pledges, which he/she must come to acknowledge as such with maturity of will and understanding.[14] The doubly representative action of the godparents, in which both the assembled church and the infant candidate participate, is not merely legal, political, or social, but spiritual: a unitive action of Christ's Spirit.

While the liturgy does not clarify the precise nature of the infant's participation in the godparents' pledging, it does affirm the mediating role of the Holy Spirit, and in so doing warns us against undue preoccupation with, or skepticism about, the capacity of the very immature to respond. At the same time, it gives proper weight to the temporal, social-moral dimension of the godparents' pledging: to the pastoral and catechetical responsibilities involved in preparing the candidate, over the course of his/her youth, for the self-conscious appropriation of his/her baptismal promises in the public rite of Confirmation. There is an implicit understanding that neglect of these "duties" of Christian nurturing may impede completion of the Spirit's work of "incorporation."

(2) *The Conformity of Common Worship to the Outer Rule of Scripture.* The English liturgies show that the obedient proclamation of worship conforms to the outer rule of Scripture as the authoritative revelation of God's judgments and actions toward his creatures. The obedient act of worship is the primary moral act of the faithful subject because it most directly represents in human speech and action God's word in Jesus Christ, spoken through the Scriptural writings, fulfilling Christ's commandments to his disciples to preach, to pray, to baptize, and to remember his saving sacrifice of himself by partaking of bread and wine.

The liturgies recognize the rule of Scripture both by taking much of their speech directly from the vernacular Scriptures, and by giving a central place to the reading of Scripture.[15] The services of Morning and

14. The service concludes with this final exhortation to the godparents: "Forasmuch as these children have promised by you to forsake the devil and all his works, to believe in God, and to serve him: you must remember that it is your parts and duties to see that these infants be taught so soon as they shall be able to learn what a solemn vow, promise and profession they have made by you." (The godparents' weighty duties are then spelled out.) *BCP*, 276.

15. Like the continental reformers, Cranmer set the Scriptural canon (as the uniquely authoritative witness in human words to God's self-revelation to his people) against all "merely human traditions," written or unwritten. In numerous places, he publically laid down the sufficiency of Holy Scripture as containing the whole of God's truth for

Evening Prayer, intended by Cranmer to be daily offices for laity as well as clergy, repeat the words of Scripture in said or sung psalms, canticles, the Lord's Prayer, and other prayers. At the same time they include lengthy, sequential readings from both Testaments. To ensure that the bulk of the Bible would be read in canonical order, Cranmer rearranged the lectionary according to the civil calendar rather than the liturgical year, so that the Old Testament would be largely covered in the course of one year, the New Testament (excepting the Apocalypse) every four months,[16] and the Psalter every month.[17]

In making Scripture-reading the centerpiece of public worship, Cranmer understood that attending to the authoritative speech of Scripture as the vehicle of divine speech, was paradigmatic of the receptivity of divine and human meanings and intentions required by all moral judgment. Cranmer and his Anglican successors asserted, unequivocally, the priority of Scripture-reading to preaching in public worship, defending it against increasingly virulent Presbyterian and Separatist objections. They insisted that human proclamation had to wait on the promise of God's self-revelation through his chosen voices: the act of congregational listening had to precede that of clerical interpretation.[18]

---

humankind and all things necessary for salvation, and as having self-interpretative power, its 'certain' meanings interpreting the 'uncertain' ones. For Cranmer the writing and arranging of the Scriptural books and the fixing of the canon by the early church was one unique work over time of the Holy Spirit. Cranmer's positions are in line with those of John Wyclif in his massive treatise of 1378, *De Veritate Sacrae Scripturae*.

16. The Apocalypse was read selectively on particular liturgical occasions.

17. In his *Preface* to the 1549 prayer book, Cranmer laid down the purpose of the church's "Common Prayers" or "Divine Service," as recognized by the "ancient Fathers," to be the ordered (sequential) reading of Holy Scripture, without interruption, repetition, or unnecessary embellishment. Accordingly, he had removed from the services of Morning and Evening Prayer (as from the first part of the Communion service) many of the non-biblical elements interleaved with the biblical, as they appeared in the earlier liturgies. Cranmer's reforms, and, indeed, his preface, owed a considerable debt to a revised Breviary produced in 1535 by Cardinal Quiñones, Franciscan Minister General, on the commission of Pope Paul III.

18. Later Elizabethan divines such as John Whitgift and Richard Hooker were forcefully articulating the Cranmerian view when they construed the disciplined reading of the whole Scripture in the church's worship as the first part of her chief corporate duty of preaching, of publishing abroad God's saving truth in Christ. To read God's written word, Hooker proposed, was to publish his self-revelation "by way of testimony" or "mere relation," which preceded and took precedence over the unfolding of its hidden mysteries by way of careful exposition of the biblical text—the second part of preaching. *Laws of Ecclesiastical Polity*, Bk. 5, ch. 19.1; Whitgift, *The Defence of the Answer to the*

For Cranmer, the canonical order of Scripture rendered it a progressive revelation of God's creative and saving purposes, and so also informed the character and elements of human good works. Cranmer recognized that scriptural revelation began with the divinely-given totality of finite beings and goods in their ordered relationships to their Creator and to one another, and that this revelation was presupposed by all subsequent revelation of God's judgments and actions in his dealings with the world and humankind. Striking in the canticles of Morning Prayer, for example, is the attention paid to God's revelation of his majesty and glory, goodness and mercy in bringing forth and sustaining the ordered totality of creatures (the *Te Deum laudamus, Benedicite omnia opera Domini Domino* [Song of the Three Young Men, vv. 35–68], and *Jubilate Deo* [Ps 100]).[19] Nevertheless, Cranmer followed his continental mentors in giving liturgical priority to God's explicit commandments as disclosing the moral implications of all his recorded judgments and actions. Moreover, the regular prayers of the church display Christ's commandments, interpreted within the whole of his ministry, as the hermeneutical key to the totality of divine commandments, and so, to the Bible as the external rule of Christian morality.[20]

For Cranmer and his liturgical circle, Christ's commandments are the authoritative disclosure of God's law given with the creation, the sure revelation of perfect human conformity, inward and outward, to God's eternal will. They do not supersede, but fulfill and interpret, God's previous revelations to Israel of the order of created beings and ends, the shared goods and structures of human community, the right relations of human beings to God, to one another, and to non-human creation.[21] All previous

---

Admonition, Tract 13, ch. 2. 1st division, *Works* vol. 3, 39–40.

19. In Evening Prayer, by contrast, praise and thanksgiving are concentrated on God's work of salvation: e.g., *Magnificat* (Luke 1:46–55), *Cantate domino* (Ps 98), *Nunc dimittis* (Luke 2:29–32).

20. Like Luther and Calvin, Cranmer, the theologian, eschewed ontological speculations, based on revealed order, as the groundwork of ethical reflection. Nor did he apparently interest himself, as did later Anglican divines such as John Whitgift and Richard Hooker, in the complex variety of modes in which divine judgments elicit and determine human moral judgments in the written and spoken Scriptural text.

21. This view controls Cranmer's "Homily Of Good Works Annexed Unto Faith" published in the official 1547 collection of Edward VI for regular use in church pulpits, to counter biblical illiteracy and theological ignorance among the preaching clergy. Here his summary of the law of Christ displays a traditional dependence on Christ's critical exchanges with the Pharisees and on his exhortations to perfection in the Sermons on the Mount and on the Plain. God's will, Cranmer tells us, is that we should surrender

revelations have their historical *telos* in the revelation of God's suffering and triumphant self-giving in his incarnate Son, true God and true man, for the salvation of his creation, and so must be interpreted as anticipations of this final revelation of moral community. Christ's precepts to his disciples are a practical commentary on this final divine-human reality.[22]

Cranmer's evangelical commandment ethic is reflected in the structure of the 1552 Eucharistic liturgy, which opens with the Lord's Prayer and a rehearsal of the Decalogue. The company of the faithful is gathered by the public proclamation of its common rule, and by a common petition for its true and spiritual keeping. But such a keeping of God's law is only open

ourselves wholly to him, trust in his promises, "love him in prosperity and adversity, and dread to offend him." For his sake, we should "love all men, friends and foes," be solicitous for their welfare and only do them good, because they are created in his image and redeemed by Christ, as we are. We should not only obey our "superiors and governors . . . for conscience sake," but seek "to serve them faithfully and diligently," likewise, we should honor our fathers and mothers with unstinting attention to their wants and wishes, as well as obedience to their demands. We should never oppress, kill, beat, slander, nor hate any man; but love, help, succor and speak well of all, even those who slander and hurt us. We should not steal or covet our neighbor's goods, but content ourselves with what we justly receive, and bestow our goods charitably, as the need of others requires. We should "commit no manner of adultery, fornication, nor unchasteness, in will as in deed." And so on. Cox, *Miscellaneous Writings*, 148–49.

22. Cranmer's christocentric commandment ethic is an ethic of "evangelical law" that has deep roots in the late-medieval Augustinian tradition as represented in the English context by John Wyclif and espoused in the 1520s and early 30s by William Tyndale under Lutheran influence. The English ethic lends a particular nuance to the Reformation dialectic of law and gospel as the controlling principle of biblical interpretation. While recognizing the generic meaning of "the law" as "the ministration of death," of God's wrathful condemnation of the sinner that drives him to repentance and faith in Christ's promises of pardon and favor, it also recognizes the indispensable role of the law within the gospel's "ministration of life." The law, says Cranmer, is the pathway of the faithful to Christ's eternal kingdom: it is intrinsic to the inward and outward, individual and communal, obedience wrought by the Spirit of the risen Christ. For the inward obedience of the faithful is their "consent to the law," their consuming desire to fulfill it, and sorrow over their shortcomings; outward obedience is the visible conformity of their action, albeit insufficient, to what Christ commands, by word and example. See: Cox, *Miscellaneous Writings*, 135–49. Cranmer's conception of the functioning of law within faith has close affinities to Melanchthon's and Calvin's explications of its pedagogical use; but Cranmer is more wholly positive about the operation of Christ's law "in the hearts" of believers than either Melanchthon or Calvin, who associate it with the continuance of "weakness and sin" (Melanchthon) in the repentant believer and the need for "a whip to the flesh," a "constant stimulus, pricking [the believer] forward when he would indulge in sloth" (Calvin). Manschreck, *Melanchthon on Christian Doctrine*, ch. 7, and reproduced in O'Donovan and O'Donovan, *From Irenaeus to Grotius*, 658; Calvin, *Institutes*, bk. 2, ch. 7.12.

to those who penitently confess their past failings, ask God's forgiveness and deliverance from their "manifold sins and wickedness," and partake of the memorial of Christ's death upon the cross, in obedience to his commandment, as the effectual sign of their incorporation into his "full, perfect and sufficient sacrifice . . . for the sins of the whole world."[23] It is in this assurance of being "very members incorporate in [Christ's] mystical body," which is the fellowship of the Holy Spirit that they beseech their heavenly Father's assistance to "do all such good works as thou hast prepared for us to walk in."[24]

(3) *The Conformity of Common Worship to the Inner Rule of the Holy Spirit.* The Eucharistic liturgies display in their structure and prayers the correspondence between the external determination of renewed moral agency and action by the rule of Christ revealed in the Scriptures, and their inner determination by the promised rule of the Holy Spirit, through which the moral subject participates in the freedom and lordship of the risen and ascended Savior. This is freedom not only from the law's condemnation of past sins, but from the oppressiveness of the law's present demands, encountered as external and alien constraints on the subject's willing and acting. The promised rule of the Spirit makes present to the faithful the lordship over the law inhering in Christ's perfect obedience to his Father's will, in which true human knowledge is wedded to proportionate and appropriate desires and affections.

As the seasonal collects of the communion service eloquently express,[25] the Spirit will make Christ's lordship present to the faithful, moment by moment, by particular operations, illumining their judgments, strengthening their resolution, generating appropriate desires and affections, bringing about effectual action in that unique succession of moral situations that comprises their individual and communal histories.[26] Exemplary is Cran-

23. *BCP*, 263.

24. Ibid., 265.

25. These are the set prayers that Cranmer himself composed, or selected and freely translated from the Latin of the Sarum Missal, i.e., the Mass book conforming to the usage of Salisbury (Sarum) Cathedral, which came to prevail in medieval Britain. They form a threefold sequence with the Epistle and Gospel readings for the day.

26. For example, the collect for Easter Day, translated from the Sarum *Processionales*: "Almighty God, which through thy only-begotten Son, Jesus Christ, hast overcome death and opened unto us the gate of everlasting life: We humbly beseech thee, that, as by thy special grace preventing us, thou dost put into our minds good desires, so by thy continual help, we may bring the same to good effect; through Jesus Christ, who liveth and reigneth with thee and the Holy Ghost, ever one God, world without end." (To be

mer's own composition for the Fourth Sunday after Easter: "Almighty God, which dost make the minds of all faithful men to be of one will: Grant unto thy people, that they may love the thing which thou commandest, and desire that which thou dost promise; that among the sundry and manifold changes of the world, our hearts may surely there be fixed, where true joys are to be found; through Jesus Christ our Lord."[27] In the promised renewal of the moral subject, there is no disjunction between knowing and willing, reason and desire, the will and the affections, the different virtues; neither is there conflict between the moral judgments of individuals, or between individual and communal judgments; for the Spirit's gift of the freedom and love of Christ is the unifying thread of the individual as of the common moral life, "the very bond of peace and all virtues," in the words of another Cranmerian collect.[28]

The christocentric and pneumatological ethic of the English liturgies takes seriously the petition of our Savior's prayer: "Thy kingdom come. Thy will be done in earth as it is in heaven." For it sets forth as a present hope a communion of persons whose equality resides in their liberty, and their liberty in their single obedience to God's will. The double rule of the Christian moral life requires recognition of the equal standing of believers as recipients of Christ's promises: it is as fellow sharers, even now, in the external rule of God's revealed word and in the internal rule of Christ's Spirit of freedom and love that the faithful are, individually, empowered and obliged to proclaim God's judgments to one another through preaching, teaching, interceding, exhorting, consoling and counseling, exercising moral judgment on their neighbor's behalf as well as for themselves. In all these acts the faithful stand along side one another as equal beneficiaries of God's merciful and saving judgments; they do not stand above their fellows, exercising condemnatory judgment on them.[29] They also stand along side

followed by Col 3:1–7; John 20:1–10.) *BCP*, 152–53; Dudley, *The Collect in Anglican Liturgy*, 73; also Armitage, *A History of the Collects*, 67.

27. *BCP*, 163; Dudley, *Collect in Anglican Liturgy*, 75–76; Armitage, *History of the Collect*, 90. The revised (1662) collect begins: "O Almighty God, who alone canst order the unruly wills and affections of sinful men."

28. *BCP*, 106.

29. The firm foothold of the English liturgical ethic in Christ's resurrection promises is an antidote to all attempts to interpret God's prior revelations of moral community in rationalistic, self-contained systems, whether of principles, ends, virtues or practices cut off from their eschatological *telos*. Likewise it is an antidote to abstract and naturalistic conceptions of the equal moral authority of human beings.

those who have not yet heard or received God's saving judgment in Christ, whom they are commissioned as servants of the Spirit's work, to gather into the community of proclamation.

Public Worship and Public Judgment

In displaying the eschatological determination of human moral agency and action by God's word of judgment given in Jesus Christ, the church's public worship is not silent about the secular determination of moral community by the practices of public judgment. On the contrary, Cranmer and his associates saw public worship as defining and empowering the secular practices of governing and being governed. The church's central liturgical act of such defining and empowering is the ordered reading of Scripture, which provides the ultimate measure, not only of true proclamation, but of just public judgment in church and commonwealth, no human judgment having validity that is repugnant to God's revealed judgments.

For Cranmer, as for the mainstream of English reforming divines, the authority, purposes and limitations of public judgment, as well as the principles of communal right, justice, and obligation, have been decisively revealed to God's chosen people: to the "Old Israel" by God's appointed giver and interpreters of his law, and to the "New Israel" by the example, commands, and judgments of Christ and his apostles.[30] But while they looked to the Israelite polity of the Old Testament, especially the united monarchy, for the authoritative model of the supreme governor's unitary jurisdiction over both the clerical and lay estates of the commonweal, they did not accept the unity of proclamation and judgment that it represented.

Rather they construed the ruler's active public judgment, whether in ecclesiastical or civil polity, to operate at the boundary of proclamatory community, at the site where moral judgment and action have broken down or are breaking down and giving way to disordered judgments, passions and affections.[31] Thus, the prayer for "Christ's Church militant" in

---

30. Late scholastic and renaissance theories of natural law (right, justice), which gave epistemological priority to unassisted reason over biblical revelation, were not much in evidence among Cranmer's clerical reforming colleagues, despite their penetration of humanist and legal circles.

31. The supreme governor's acts of judgment were both retrospective and prospective responses to human wrongdoing: on the one hand, the ruler judged particular (individual or collective) acts retrospectively to be violations of right and derelictions of specific duties binding on all within his/her jurisdiction; and on the other, he/she defined

the communion service characteristically beseeches God that the Queen's "whole Council" and "all that be put in authority under her . . . may truly and indifferently minister justice, to the punishment of wickedness and vice, and to the maintenance of God's true religion and virtue."[32] Typically, official sermons of the period portray the "godly order" of the common-weal as requiring that "kings and governors" be the "common revengers, correctors and reformers of all common and private things that be amiss," executing "the right judgment of God's wrath against sin" for the common benefit.[33]

The official sermons display an understanding of coercive public judg-ments as incomplete or deficient representations of God's judgments; they are deficient in that they represent only God's condemnation of sin and his merciful preservation of sinful human community against its ravages, but not his saving, judgments toward his creatures. They cannot re-present the judgment of Christ's suffering and triumphant love that justifies and regen-erates the contrite sinner. Although they may furnish the context and even the external form of "correction," they do not accomplish the inward recon-ciliation and communion of formerly antagonistic wills, which is promised to those who participate, through faith, in Christ's resurrection life.[34]

---

in law particular types of acts as violations of right and derelictions of specific duties, presumed or stated. In addition, he/she appointed to public posts and distributed public and private honors and benefits, under the rationale of giving justice, sustaining social order and preventing controversy. The law of the land arose through these three sets of authoritative judgments: judicial, legislative, and administrative.

32. *BCP*, 254.

33. "A Sermon Concerning the Time of Rebellion," in Cox, *Miscellaneous Writings*, 193. Cranmer wrote this sermon in collaboration with Peter Martyr and preached it at St. Pauls, London (July, 1549) in the wake of religious and economic uprisings.

34. Running through Cranmer's sermon against rebellion is an implicit contrast be-tween the prophetic judgment on sin spoken by the preacher, and the political judgment on crime enacted by the ruler, as diverging representations of divine wrath. Whereas the former proclamation never separates God's wrath against sin from his saving purposes in Christ, and so is a direct instrument of the Spirit's work of repentance, faith, and re-generation, the latter necessarily does, yet not to the point of denying God's patience and mercy in sustaining the sinful human community, including both wrongdoers and those wronged. In executing justice, terminating conflict, punishing offenders and vindicating those offended against, the ruler is, at most, a remote instrument of the Spirit's saving work. E.g., Cranmer's *Sermon concerning the Time of Rebellion* is a sustained prophetic condemnation of the vice on both sides of the conflict, and call to repentance, and at the same time; it is an unambiguous statement of the remit of political authority. Cox, *Miscellaneous Writings*, 190–202.

Nevertheless, despite the manifold deficiencies of public judgments, which the English reformers discuss at some length,[35] the English liturgies show them as *serving* the church's proclamation of God's judgments in their trinitarian fullness. In the sphere of church polity (including liturgical practice), they are seen chiefly to curb the more subtle spiritual vices of moral and intellectual pride, which cause believers, without sufficient biblical warrant, to pit their own judgments against common judgment, disrupting the seemly order of common practice and breaking the bond of communal peace.[36] While the requirement of conformity or uniform practice is impotent, of itself, to bring about conversion of the subject's heart and growth in virtue, it may, by compelling individual conceit to defer to outward unity and concord, be an extraneous instrument of the Spirit's proper action. So subjects pray for the blessing of being "godly and quietly governed" (again, the prayer for Christ's church militant). Only, however, by the Spirit's guidance may they come to "obey gladly" a common policy with which they do not agree, for the sake of sustaining communal peace and good order.

Conclusion

In the preceding, I have attempted to show the Cranmerian Book of Common Prayer to be the core theological articulation of an English reformation ethical and political legacy that continues to deserve our attention. In the midst of the legalistic and juridical ethos of contemporary liberal society, interpenetrated as it is with the technological project of mastering human and non-human nature, we stand in fresh need of the English reformers' insight into the diverse ways in which the constitutive practices of church and civil government, those of evangelical proclamation and coercive judgment, determine and govern human moral agency and action. We need

35. The seminal text for this discussion was Thomas Starkey's *Exhortation to Unity and Obedience* (London: c. 1540), which owes a great deal to Thomas Aquinas's discussion of human law in *ST* 1a2ae.95.2.

36. The English reformers understood that it is precisely the relative arbitrariness of human laws and regulations that provokes proud dissent among the ruled: that is, dissent not truly required by God's revealed judgments. The great debate of the later Elizabethan church concerned whether aspects of legislated church polity were or were not in conformity with God's revealed judgments; for both sides agreed that God neither requires nor permits subjects to suspend their own judgment about what common action is commanded and allowed by his just laws.

to be especially reminded that only the eschatological renewal of human moral agency and action, through the church's practice of proclamation, centered in her common worship, can overcome the tyranny of the law in all its social and psychological manifestations; because this renewal is our incorporation, even now, into the community of Christ's divine-human obedience, which is his lordship over and fulfillment of God's law. The church's practice of common worship extends to those who have died with Christ the possibility of proclaiming in their moral judgments the history of God's own creative and saving judgments in his Son.

The Cranmerian liturgies show us how the obedient act of worship is paradigmatic for renewed moral agency and action by displaying, in a theologically reflexive manner, its christological basis, its eschatological communal subject, its outer rule by God's revealed word, and its inner rule by the Spirit of Christ. They also show us how the freedom of Christ's resurrection community orders and sustains the freedom of fallen humanity to participate in the created order of human goods, albeit in a distorted and fragmentary way, and its freedom to protect and sustain that participation through coercive public judgment (our political freedom). In this way they define and empower the determination of moral community by public judgment. But this role of common worship depends on its publicity, an aspect of which has been its recognition in public law as the action of the one, holy, catholic, and apostolic church. This dialectical relationship between proclamation and public judgment continues to warrant careful probing today; and our response to the various forms of civil-church establishments, both long-standing and emerging in our contemporary world, should not be one of dogmatic rejection, on the legalistic and juridical grounds of egalitarian religious rights, as is all too common in advanced liberal polities, but one of critical receptivity to the longer Christian tradition.

4

Richard Hooker on the
Book of Common Prayer

ROGER BECKWITH

Note. When I became warden of Latimer House, Oxford, in 1973, after serving for ten years as librarian under Dr. Jim Packer and John Wenham, the first librarian who came to assist me was Peter Toon. He stayed until 1976, since when Peter and I have sought to collaborate in other ways. When he came he was chiefly known as a church historian, but while at Latimer House he began those studies of liturgy, and especially of the Book of Common Prayer, to which he has since devoted so much attention. It was also there that he began working for his Oxford DPhil, which he achieved the year after he left. When at Latimer House, Peter and Vita did not yet have children of their own, but Janet and I had three young sons, and one of their happy recollections of their childhood is of Peter kindly organizing cricket for them on the large lawn behind Latimer House, taking them out strawberry-picking, and advertising a conker-competition for them, which concluded with Kentucky Fried Chicken.

The great pioneer of the Reformation of the Church of England was of course Thomas Cranmer. As archbishop of Canterbury he was in a unique position to fill this role, and as a man of simple faith, genuine learning, cautious judgment, and unique liturgical gifts, he filled it astonishingly well. But a reformation required not only pioneers but also expositors and defenders, and the next generation produced just such a man in Richard Hooker. Among the strictly theological writers of the Church of England, there is none who holds a higher place, or perhaps so high a place, as Hooker. It was his role to expound and defend the reformed settlement of the Church of England that Cranmer had pioneered, and his exposition and defense is one that has never been surpassed, and has never been effectively answered.

Hooker was born during the tyrannous reign of Mary Tudor, probably in March 1554, just two years before Cranmer suffered martyrdom at the stake for his faith. While Hooker was still a child, in 1558, Elizabeth came to the throne and restored Cranmer's work, putting it upon a permanent footing. Hooker's parents were poor, but his intellectual promise was brought to the attention of Bishop John Jewel of Salisbury, the great patristic scholar among the English Reformers, and with the bishop's help he was entered at the bishop's old college of Corpus Christi, Oxford, where he later became a fellow. His piety was as marked as was his learning. His life was peaceful and untroubled, except by poor health, and the tradition that his marriage was unhappy, reported by Izaak Walton in his famous *Life of Mr Richard Hooker*, seems not to be true.[1] He became, when he left college, a diligent parish priest, and for some years he was master of the Temple church, among the London lawyers, where he found himself in controversy with his Puritan reader, Walter Travers. The preaching there, we are told, was "pure Canterbury in the morning and Geneva in the afternoon." Hooker's final living was at Bishopsbourne, near Canterbury, where he died in November 1600, aged only forty-six.

In the preface to Dr. Johnson's *Dictionary*, he honored Hooker as one of the greatest writers in the English language. This is what he said: "The chief glory of every people arises from its authors: whether I shall add anything by my own writings to the reputation of English literature, must be left to time . . . but I shall not think my employment useless or ignoble, if by my assistance foreign nations, and distant ages, gain access to the propagators of knowledge, and understand the teachers of truth; if my labours

---

1. Sisson, *Judicious Marriage*.

afford light to the repositories of science [knowledge], and add celebrity to *Bacon*, to *Hooker*, to *Milton* and to *Boyle*."

The great reputation of Hooker began in his lifetime, and has never been higher than it is today. All schools of thought among Anglicans try to claim him as their own—the Evangelicals, because he emphasized Scripture, the Anglo-Catholics, because he emphasized tradition, and the Liberals, because he emphasized natural reason. He emphasized all three authorities, and he was making no new departure by doing so. The "Magisterial Reformers," notably Luther and Calvin, had similarly been willing to appeal to all three. It was Hooker's contemporaries, the Presbyterian Puritans, who, by trying to narrow down their appeal to Scripture alone, were making a new departure. But though he appealed to all three, Hooker did not put them on a level with each other, as Liberals often imagine, still less did he give priority to reason, or indeed to tradition. Rather, he gave an emphatic priority to Scripture. Scripture, Hooker argues, is supreme and final on all matters with which it deals (*Ecclesiastical Polity* I: 11–15). On those matters, tradition and reason may interpret and apply it, but may not oppose it.[2] At the same time, Scripture does not deal with everything, and on matters with which it does not deal we may be, and indeed ought to be, guided by reason and tradition. Even in church affairs, the Bible does not try to settle everything, and where it does not settle something, the church may legitimately make its own provisions and expect people to abide by them. Even if you think the church has decided wrongly, you should seek to abide by what it has decided until it decides otherwise.

In his own day, Hooker was arguing partly against the extreme Roman Catholics, who claimed that, in religious matters, everything should be decided by tradition and the teaching church, rather than by Scripture, but particularly against the extreme Puritans, who claimed that everything should be decided by Scripture alone, to the effective exclusion of tradition and reason. What was not in the Bible should be treated not just as unimportant but as wrong, they claimed, while what was in the Bible, even as a practice backed by no command, should be treated as mandatory. Extreme Roman Catholics had by Hooker's time withdrawn from the Church of England, but extreme Puritans were very active within it, and continued to be so until after the Commonwealth period in the mid-seventeenth

2. For a fuller discussion, see Atkinson, *Richard Hooker and the Authority of Scripture, Tradition and Reason*. For evidence that Hooker agreed with the "Magisterial Reformers" on other important issues, see Kirby, *Richard Hooker's Doctrine of the Royal Supremacy*, esp. ch. 2.

century. However, in the 1660s, with the restoration of the monarch, the bishops, and the Prayer Book, they mostly became Nonconformists.

It might be thought that Hooker's case against extreme Puritanism, however powerful, would have little relevance to us today. Yet much of it is remarkably up to date. The claims of the Puritans are not heard today in exactly the form that they were. No one now says that what is not taught in the Bible is unlawful, but many people hold that what is not taught there does not matter. True, what is not taught in the Bible is less important, but that does not mean that it is of no importance at all. Chaos results if we draw that conclusion. There are also people today who think, like the Puritans, that whatever happened in biblical times ought to happen now: They apply this to speaking in tongues, as if the Holy Spirit is not free to act in different ways in different ages. But the greatest similarity of all, probably, is that the Puritans took the law into their own hands, rather like the Anglo-Catholics in the nineteenth century. What they thought was right they went ahead and did, regardless of the Prayer Book or the accepted practice of the church. We are today in such an age once more. As in the days of the Judges, "every man does what is right in his own eyes," and the habit has spread to all schools of thought. Hooker confronted this situation, and, by his sober defense of the Prayer Book and of established practice, helps us to confront it too.

Hooker called his famous treatise *The Laws of Ecclesiastical Polity.* "Polity" means "form of government," so the laws of ecclesiastical polity are the laws of church government. Without trying to be exhaustive, it is a most comprehensive account, and in modern editions fills three large volumes, though it is divided into eight shorter books—books nearer the size that was customary in classical antiquity. It was written in the last decade of Hooker's life, and only books 1–5 were published in his lifetime. The remaining three books lacked his final revision, and were withheld from publication until after the middle of the seventeenth century, when controversy arose about their authenticity. The balance of scholarly opinion, however, is that books 7 and 8 are genuine, though there is doubt about book 6, which is incomplete.[3]

Book 1 deals with laws in general, and distinguishes their various kinds. Book 2 deals with the Puritan claim that all laws ought to be drawn from Scripture; Book 3 with the Puritan claim that there must be a form of church government laid down in Scripture, which all are obliged to follow;

3. See Houk, ed. *Hooker's Ecclesiastical Polity Book VIII*; Booty, "Quest."

and Book 4 with the Puritan claim that the Church of England retains too much of mediaeval and Roman Catholic practice. Book 5 deals with the particular objections that the Puritans make against Anglican doctrine and practice. It is here that Hooker discusses the Puritan objections to the Book of Common Prayer, so it is here that our attention in this paper will be concentrated. He also deals here with the doctrine of the sacraments and ordination. Book 6 (the incomplete book) deals with church discipline, and with the Puritan claim that there ought to be lay elders to administer it. Book 7 deals with the authority of bishops, and Book 8 with the royal supremacy in the church.

Four Propositions

Hooker begins his fifth book, which is our subject here, by establishing four general propositions (V: 5–10). He supports these propositions both by argument and by quotations from the Bible. His first proposition is that public services ought to be suitable to the greatness of the God whom we are worshipping. As he expresses it, "Duties of religion, performed by whole societies of men, ought to have in them according to our power a sensible [perceptible] excellency, correspondent to the majesty of him whom we worship" (V: 6:2). And in support of this he quotes Solomon's words about the Temple: "And the house which I build is great: for great is our God above all gods" (2 Chr 2:5). Informality may suit private devotion, but it does not, generally, suit corporate worship in public. In arguing this, Hooker of course sets himself against the main tendencies in worship that have developed in our own day.

His second proposition is that we must not lightly esteem what antiquity and the continuous practice of the church has thought suitable. The Bible values the experience of old age (Job 12:12; Ps 37:25) and of past generations (Deut 32:7), and we should do the same. This does not chime in very well with the youth culture of our own time, which tends to regard the older generation as out of touch, and anything old-fashioned as tedious, but what Hooker says may be true nonetheless.

Hooker's third proposition qualifies his second. It is this: that nevertheless, the church has authority in matters of church order, left undecided by the Bible, to make changes. Doctrine is unchangeable, but church order, in many matters, is not. And the church has more authority in those matters than private individuals have. He quotes in this connection Ecclesiastes

4:9, "two are better than one," which is not directly relevant, but his point is hard to quarrel with, just the same.

Hooker's fourth proposition is that necessity sometimes requires exceptions to be made from general rules. He quotes what Jesus said about David being right to eat the showbread, when he would otherwise have starved (Luke 6:4).

Hooker then goes on to apply these general propositions, and especially the first three, to particular matters on which the practice of the Church of England was being attacked. He begins with the criticism of its magnificent church buildings. He defends these on the lines of his first proposition, that what is great is suitable to a great God, adding that the Bible provides examples of places of worship similarly magnificent, and that Psalm 96:9 exhorts us to "worship the Lord in the beauty of holiness" (V: 11–17).

The Ministry of the Word

From the place of worship, Hooker passes on to the actual substance of services, and begins with the ministry of the word, which he notes distinguishes Christian services from pagan services, and reflects the special importance that Christianity attaches to the knowledge of God. In the ministry of the word he includes not simply sermons but the Catechism, for the instruction of children and beginners, the public reading of Scripture, as witness to the truth, and the reading of written Homilies and of selections from the Apocrypha, as explanations of Scripture. He labors this point at length (V: 18–22) because his Puritan opponents made sermons the only ordinary means of salvation; but he sets against the Puritans' proofs from Romans 10:14f. and 1 Corinthians 1:21 rival proofs from Deuteronomy 31:11–13, 2 Chronicles 34:18–21, and 2 Timothy 3:15f., to show that the public reading of Scripture, without exposition in sermons, is also spiritually effectual. He sums up his argument like this:

> The sum which truth amounteth unto will appear to be but this, that as medicines provided of nature and applied by art for the benefit of bodily health, take effect sometimes under and sometimes above the natural proportion of their virtue, according as the mind and fancy of the patient doth more or less concur with them: so whether we barely read unto men the Scriptures of God, or by homilies concerning matter of belief and conversation [behavior]

> seek to lay before them the duties which they owe unto God
> man; whether we deliver them books to read and consider
> private at their own best leisure, or call them to the heari
> sermons publicly in the house of God; albeit every of these and the
> like unto these means do truly and daily effect that in the hearts
> of men for which they are each and all meant, yet the operation
> which they have in common being most sensible and most gener-
> ally noted in one kind above the rest, that one hath in some men's
> opinions drowned altogether the rest, and injuriously brought to
> pass that they have been thought, not *less effectual* than the other,
> but without the other *uneffectual* to save souls. (V: 22:20)

As Hooker points out, much more of Scripture can be read in the
lessons than can be expounded in sermons, and therefore it ought to be
read, so that the congregation may learn. Of course, Hooker wrote at a time
when more than half the population was illiterate, and it would have been
useless to tell such people to read the Bible for themselves. Nowadays, sadly,
though nobody is illiterate, exhortations to Christians to read the Bible for
themselves still seem often to fall upon deaf ears. The greatest privilege of
being able to read is being able to read the Bible, and we ought to think any
day a missed opportunity when we do not read some part of it. Even so, we
will still be profited by hearing it read to us in church as well, and by hearing some part of it expounded.

Prayer

From the ministry of the word, Hooker passes on to prayer, and so begins
on the actual spoken text of the Book of Common Prayer. It is here that his
admiration for Cranmer's liturgy becomes explicit.

> A great part of the cause (he writes), wherefore religious minds are
> so inflamed with the love of public devotion, is that virtue, force,
> and efficacy, which by experience they find that the very form and
> reverend solemnity of common prayer duly ordered hath, to help
> that imbecility and weakness in us, by means whereof we are oth-
> erwise of ourselves the less apt to perform unto God so heavenly a
> service, with such affection of heart, and disposition in the powers
> of our souls as is requisite. To this end therefore all things here-
> unto appertaining have been ever thought convenient to be done
> with the most solemnity and majesty that the wisest could devise.
> It is not with public as with private prayer. In this rather secrecy is

> commended than outward show, whereas that being the public act
> of a whole society, requireth more care to be had of external ap-
> pearance. The very assembling of men therefore unto this service
> hath been ever solemn.

And again:

> But of all helps for the due performance of this service the greatest
> is that very set and standing order itself, which framed with com-
> mon advice, hath both for matter and form prescribed whatever
> is herein publicly done. No doubt from God it hath proceeded,
> and by us it must be acknowledged a work of his singular care
> and providence, that the Church hath evermore held a prescript
> form of common prayer, although not in all things everywhere
> the same, yet for the most part retaining still the same analogy. So
> that if the liturgies of all ancient churches throughout the world be
> compared amongst themselves, it may be easily perceived they had
> all one original mould, and that the public prayers of the people of
> God in churches thoroughly settled did never use to be voluntary
> dictates proceeding from any man's extemporal wit. (V: 25:1, 4)

Hooker was writing less than fifty years after Cranmer had compiled
the first English liturgy, yet already he is ranking it with the treasures of
antiquity.

The use of the Psalms as vehicles of prayer was something the Puritans
criticized. As they are parts of Scripture, the Puritans complained that they
were read in a different way from the rest of Scripture, and more frequently.
Hooker's reply to this carping charge is eloquent:

> They are not ignorant what difference there is between other
> parts of Scripture and Psalms. The choice and flower of all things
> profitable in other books the Psalms do both more briefly contain,
> and more movingly also express, by reason of that poetical form
> wherewith they are written. The ancients when they speak of the
> Book of Psalms use to fall into large discourses, shewing how this
> part above the rest doth of purpose set forth and celebrate all the
> considerations and operations which belong to God; it magnifi-
> eth the holy meditations and actions of divine men; it is of things
> heavenly an universal declaration, working in them whose hearts
> God inspireth with the true consideration thereof, an habit or dis-
> position of mind whereby they are made fit vessels both for receipt
> and for delivery of whatsoever spiritual perfection. What is there
> necessary for man to know which the Psalms are not able to teach?
> They are to beginners an easy and familiar introduction, a mighty

augmentation of all virtue and knowledge in such as are entered before, a strong confirmation to the most perfect among others. Heroical magnanimity, exquisite justice, grave moderation, exact wisdom, repentance unfeigned, unwearied patience, the mysteries of God, the sufferings of Christ, the terrors of wrath, the comforts of grace, the works of Providence over this world, and the promised joys of that world which is to come, all good necessarily to be either known or done or had, this one celestial fountain yieldeth. Let there be any grief or disease incident into the soul of man, any wound or sickness named, for which there is not in this treasure-house a present comfortable remedy at all times ready to be found. Hereof it is that we covet to make the Psalms especially familiar unto all. This is the very cause why we iterate the Psalms oftener than any other part of Scripture besides; the cause wherefore we inure the people together with their minister, and not the minister alone to read them as other parts of Scripture he doth. (V: 37:2)

Hooker then proceeds with equal eloquence to justify the use of music with the Psalms (V: 38).

In addition, the Puritans objected to the antiphonal recitation of Psalms, Canticles, and Prayers, as being found in the Old Testament but not in the New. This frivolous charge Hooker rebuts, and points to the value of antiphonal recitation as involving both priest and people in the joint presentation of their petitions and devotions (V: 39).

Rather absurdly, the Puritans objected to the comprehensive supplication that we call the Litany, on the grounds that some of the dangers it prays God to avert are less immediate than others (V: 41). The Puritans doubtless disliked the Litany because of its antiphonal form, which to Hooker was, of course, a merit.

Objection was also made to the frequency with which the Lord's Prayer occurs in the Prayer Book services. This is an undeniable fact, and the answer Hooker makes to the criticism is interesting. He says that since Christ gave us his prayer not only as a prayer to use but also as a model for our prayers, it is a good idea to bring the model before our minds fairly often, to prevent them straying too far away from it (V: 35).

Miscellaneous Topics

The Puritans objected likewise to various ceremonial customs: they objected to the wearing of the surplice, which Hooker defends as harmless and decent (V: 29); they objected to standing for the Gospel rather than for other parts of Scripture, which he defends on the grounds that the Gospel contains the very acts and words of Jesus (V: 30:3); they objected to the sign of the cross in baptism and the use of the ring in marriage, which he defends as significant and useful customs (V: 65, 73). None of these ceremonies is mentioned in Scripture, so the Puritans disliked them for that reason in particular. For the same reason they objected to the observance of any festival days except the Lord's Day, Sunday, which the New Testament mentions: but Hooker replies that this is no good ground for objecting, and that the revolution of the year almost compels us to observe times and seasons, which can be very edifying (V: 71).

At infant baptism, the Puritans objected to the answering of the questions about faith and repentance by proxy. In answer, Hooker points out that baptism is the sacrament of faith, and that the godparents are only anticipating the faith that the infants will one day, hopefully, express for themselves (V: 64).

Finally, the Puritans objected to five phrases that are used at different points in the Prayer Book. It is astonishing really that such captious critics could not find more than five to object to, but these objections also Hooker patiently answers (V: 44–49). One of them concerns the request in the Litany for deliverance from "sudden death," and what this means, he explains, is unprepared death.

Confirmation and Ordination

Hooker spends much space on the doctrine of the two sacraments, which he suspects the Puritans of undervaluing, and he deals positively also with the related ceremonies of confirmation and ordination. Confirmation he views as an act of blessing, in which the bishop prays for the gift of the Holy Spirit, given in baptism, to be further strengthened (V: 66). Ordination he deals with at greater length and attributes to it great importance. Section 76 is entitled "Of the nature of that Ministry which serveth for performance of divine duties in the Church of God, and how happiness not eternal only but also temporal doth depend upon it." The reason why ministers have this prerogative right, above all others, to perform divine duties is ordination, in which a gift of the Holy Spirit is conferred (V: 77). This gift is sometimes spoken of in the New Testament as various gifts, but there are only two ordained *offices*, presbyters and deacons, the bishops being senior presbyters, like the apostles before them (V: 78). This somewhat surprising but thought-provoking account of the ministry is further developed in book 7, which is devoted to the authority of bishops.

The Sacraments

With regard to the two sacraments, baptism and Holy Communion, the point which Hooker constantly emphasizes is that they are true means of grace. In this, of course, Hooker is simply underlining the statements of the Prayer Book and the Thirty-Nine Articles. He has already fully conceded that the ministry of the word is a means of grace, a doctrinal instrument of salvation, effectual to save souls; but he is concerned that the Puritans assimilate the operation of the sacraments so closely to that of the word (in both cases teaching the mind), as to make them seem superfluous. Besides, if they simply teach the mind, how can baptism benefit unconscious infants, he asks? (V: 57:1). The sacraments must have a necessity of their own. He locates this necessity in that they are marks of God's bestowal of saving grace on all who are capable thereof, and are conditions required if they are to receive it (V: 57:3).

Hooker has included at this point an extended discussion of the doctrine of the incarnation (V: 51–55). The Christ with whom we are united through the word and Sacraments, he points out, is not the pre-existent Christ but Christ incarnate, crucified, and risen. He is now ascended to heaven and is present with us through the Holy Spirit. The Holy Spirit unites us with Christ's divine nature, but does he also unite us with Christ's human nature? His glorified body is in heaven, but since his human nature is by personal union joined to his divine nature, wherever his divinity is present, his humanity must in some mode (even though not in a local mode) be present as well. It is in this way that Hooker explains the real participation of Christ, yes, of his body and blood, in the Holy Communion. It is because he is divine that he is the Bread of Life to us, but he is also human, and he presents himself to us in both natures.

As Hooker sees it, the great divide in Eucharistic doctrine is between those who affirm a real participation of Christ by believers, through the sacrament, and those who deny it. The question of a presence *in the elements* is secondary: the real question is do those who *rightly receive* the elements receive Christ or not? He puts it like this:

This was it that some did exceedingly fear, lest Zuinglius and OEcolampadius would bring it to pass, that men should account of this sacrament but only as of a shadow, destitute, empty and void of Christ. But seeing that by opening the several opinions which have been held, they are grown for aught I can see on all sides at the length to a general agreement concerning that which alone is material, namely the *real participation* of Christ and of life in his body and blood *by means of this sacrament*; wherefore should the world continue still distracted and rent with so manifold contentions, when there remaineth now no controversy saving only about the subject *where* Christ is? Yea even in this point no side denieth but that *the soul of man* is the receptacle of Christ's presence. Whereby the question is yet driven to a narrower issue, nor doth any thing rest doubtful but this, whether when the sacrament is administered Christ be whole *within man only*, or else his body and blood be also externally seated in the very consecrated elements themselves; which opinion they that defend are driven either to *consubstantiate* and incorporate Christ with elements sacramental, or to *transubstantiate* and change their substance into his; and so the one to hold him really but invisibly moulded up with the substance of those elements, the other to hide him under the only visible show of bread and wine, the substance whereof as they imagine is abolished and his succeeded in the same room. . . .

All things considered and compared with that success which truth hath hitherto had by so bitter conflicts with errors in this point, shall I wish that men would more give themselves to meditate with silence what we have by the sacrament, and less to dispute of the manner how? (V: 67:2–3).

For his own part, Hooker is clear that transubstantiation and similar notions are wrong. His famous words on the point are these: "The real presence of Christ's most blessed body and blood is not therefore to be sought for in the sacrament, but in the worthy receiver of the sacrament" (V: 67:6)—the one who receives with repentance and faith. And in this, of course, he is only echoing the language of the Prayer Book service, where in the consecration prayer, at the heart of the service, what we ask is not for any change in the elements, but that "we may be *partakers* of his most blessed body and blood."

I hope that enough has now been said to make clear the importance of Hooker's work for lovers of the Book of Common Prayer. Hooker expounded and defended the teaching and use of the Prayer Book and set it in a broad context of theology. You cannot get away from the Prayer Book without getting away from Hooker, and no school of thought in the Anglican Church wants to do that, apparently. Hooker and Cranmer support each other, and where one flourishes the other will do so too. I regard this as a very hopeful sign for the future of the Prayer Book in our church. However much it is discriminated against at present, it will make a comeback. And Peter Toon, whose memory we here honor, would have been happy to think that this is so.

5

Recovering Confessional Anglicanism[1]

GILLIS J. HARP

"When I use a word," Humpty Dumpty said, in rather a scornful tone, "it means just what I choose it to mean—neither more nor less."

"The question is," said Alice, "whether you CAN make words mean so many different things."

"The question is," said Humpty Dumpty, "which is to be master—that's all."

—THROUGH THE LOOKING GLASS)

If the story of North American Anglicanism in the last generation has demonstrated anything, it is the catastrophic consequences of ignoring our Reformation formularies. Forgetting the Thirty-Nine Articles has, of course, been part of a larger assault on traditional doctrine. Relegating the Articles to the "Historical Documents" section of the 1979 American BCP was a small part of this shift but a revealing one nonetheless. As the costly results of a nonconfessional Anglicanism continue to work themselves out in the Episcopal Church and in the Anglican Church of Canada, orthodox Anglicans have homework to do. We need to revisit the Reformation formularies,

1. Re-published with permission of *The Churchman*, Autumn, 2002.

study them afresh, and work to restore them to a central place in the teaching and life of whatever orthodox body emerges from the current mess. A critical part of this study is learning how to interpret the Articles correctly in the wake of decades of misinterpretation and obfuscation.

My approach in the following essay is both descriptive (surveying quickly some of the history of interpretation) and also prescriptive; that is, arguing for what I think is the most responsible, historically-informed and fruitful way to read, understand, and apply the Articles today.

Although I have long been an amateur student of the Articles, I confess that I have become more keen about them in recent years. Like many Anglican evangelicals, I have long been an admirer of the Westminster Standards, particularly the Shorter Catechism. My recent interaction with conservative confessional Presbyterians has convinced me of several things. One, the standards of preaching in the Episcopal Church at large are abysmal. Two, the practice of biblical discipline in most Episcopal congregations (even "evangelical" ones) is virtually unknown. Three (and more to the point here), the Westminster Standards, despite their many virtues, are occasionally too detailed and precise about secondary matters. This feature of Presbyterian confessional standards has created problems within conservative Presbyterian circles. Read about the current arguments within the Orthodox Presbyterian Church (OPC) and the Presbyterian Church in America (PCA) regarding the Confession's wording about the days of creation (were they twenty-four hour periods or not? etc.) and you will understand my point. I would argue that the Articles' brevity is a wonderful virtue (note here that I said brevity and *not* ambiguity—on the core issues, the Articles are decidedly not ambiguous, as we shall see). The Articles (along with the classic 1662 BCP) are one of Anglicanism's great treasures.

The Articles of Religion were a product of the English Reformation and, in their final form, of one particular phase of that Reformation, the Elizabethan Settlement. As such, they naturally reflect the concerns of the Reformation era, in addition to affirming the creedal bedrock laid in the first five centuries of the history of the Christian church. Philip Schaff best summarized the main characteristics of the Articles long ago: "[They] are Catholic in the ecumenical doctrines of the Holy Trinity and the Incarnation," especially drawing upon the Lutheran Augsburg and Wurtemberg Confessions. "They are Augustinian in the anthropological and soteriological doctrines of free-will, sin and grace. . . . They are Protestant and evangelical in rejecting the peculiar errors and abuses of Rome. . . . They are Reformed or moderately Calvinistic in the two doctrines of Predestination and the Lord's Supper . . . [and] they are Erastian in the political section." Hence the Articles' original historical context is the sixteenth-century Protestant Reformation, and not just the English Reformation but the Continental Reformation as well. Schaff wrote that the Articles taught "those doctrines of Scripture and tradition, justification by faith, faith and good works, the Church, and the number of the sacraments, which Luther, Zwingli and Calvin held in common."[2]

If one is seeking to define clearly Anglican identity in this muddled age, one is met, then, with a major obstacle at the outset. The vast majority of American Episcopal layfolk (and, in my experience, many of its clergy) are woefully ignorant of the Reformation. If the defining documents of Anglicanism, the Reformation formularies (Articles, BCP, Ordinal, and Homilies) are products of an era that most Anglicans know little or nothing about, we do have a problem. And the problem is not solely one of ignorance but of unease or downright hostility. Episcopalians are embarrassed about Henry VIII. Many take pride in the fact that Anglicans broke with Rome but "avoided Luther's extremes" (whatever that is supposed to mean!). I have been astonished at how other churches of the magisterial Reformation show a much greater knowledge of, and appreciation for, their Reformation roots. Lutherans and Presbyterians celebrate Reformation Sunday and sing "A mighty fortress" with gusto. Why shouldn't Anglicans do so also? Episcopalians seem vaguely embarrassed by it all. In the ECUSA calendar, the Oxford martyrs are lumped together in a single day— yet is it ever observed in Episcopal churches? (At least in Canada and England, Cranmer has his own day and Latimer and Ridley appropriately share one.) Much of this myopia regarding the Reformation stems from the Tractarian movement and its Anglo-Catholic successors, but one must frankly recognize it as a serious problem undermining the recovery of authentic Anglicanism in North America.

J. I. Packer and Roger Beckwith have ably refuted the old saw that the Articles are ambiguous and equivocal. On the main points of contention with Roman Catholicism they are indeed crystal clear. Scripture is clearly identified as the supreme rule of faith and other essential matters follow: the fact of human depravity; the biblical understanding of justification (what Luther aptly labeled the doctrine on which the church stands or falls); the doctrine of assurance; the meaning and purpose of the

2. Schaff quoted by Hankey, "The Thirty-Nine Articles as a Theological System," 4.

sacraments. On the flip side of the coin, they are also admirably clear in their negative teaching—i.e., their rejection of medieval tenets: purgatory, transubstantiation, denying the cup to the laity, the sacrifice of the Mass, and several others. What one often forgets is that they are also very clear about which Anabaptist distinctives they repudiate: Pelagianism, deprecating the sacraments, rejecting infant baptism, inattention to the order of the church visible, and other matters. Indeed, often what strikes us as an odd turn of phrase has its roots in a point arising from Anabaptist teaching.[3] Some Anglican evangelicals today seem to forget this side of the question; they are savage in their treatment of Rome but are strangely silent regarding serious Anabaptist errors.

As noted already, the Articles do leave many secondary matters open or unresolved. Bishop Pearson concluded in 1660 that they were not "pretended to be a complete body of divinity" but, rather "an enumeration of some truths," truths that were the minimal doctrinal requirement for those charged with the pastoral ministry in the Church of England.[4] Subscription to such a modest set of doctrines by the clergy would secure theological (and political) peace in a necessarily comprehensive national church. Of course, "comprehensive" here does not mean what Anglican liberals in the twentieth century have meant by that term.

Packer and Beckwith identify roughly three traditions of interpretation of the Articles over the centuries. They label these Reformed, Latitudinarian and Catholic. In the first group, one should include T. P. Boultbee, *A Commentary on the Thirty Nine Articles*, E. A. Litton, *Introduction to Dogmatic Theology* and, most notably, W. H. Griffith Thomas, *The Principles of Theology*. (Litton's commentary has recently been reprinted.) Perhaps the very first commentary in this Reformed tradition was Thomas Rogers, *The Catholic Doctrine Believed and Professed in the Church of England* (1607), reprinted by the Parker Society in the nineteenth century. These commentators understood most of the key Reformation issues as central to the faith and sympathized with most of the answers furnished in the Articles. Naturally, they stressed the centrality of the Articles to understanding the

---

3. I highly recommend Packer and Beckwith's superb booklet *The Thirty-Nine Articles: Their Place and Use Today*. Substantial portions of this essay are based upon this work. Calvin once wrote that some Anabaptists were "a hundred times worse and more pernicious . . . [than] the papists." (Calvin quoted by Farley, *Treatises Against the Anabaptists and Against the Libertines*. I am indebted to my colleague T. David Gordon for this reference.)

4. Pearson is quoted in Packer, *The Thirty-Nine Articles*, 37.

fundamental, doctrinal character of Anglicanism. The party battles of the nineteenth century sometimes gave them different concerns or emphases than those of the sixteenth-century Reformers, but their approach to the Articles was certainly sympathetic.

The second, or moderate latitudinarian approach, was best represented by Burnet's *Exposition of the Thirty-Nine Articles* (1699) which was popular for decades among many and not just latitudinarians (Burnet can often sound fairly high church). These commentators adopted a Whiggish view of the Reformation as a grand deliverance from the superstition of the Dark Ages, and part of a larger march of progress toward common sense and rationality. Theological liberals extended this approach at the beginning of the twentieth century. One used to encounter such an interpretation of the Reformation in high school and college textbooks that portrayed Luther as a champion of individual liberty (quite a stretch for a figure as thoroughly medieval as Luther). Sometimes one got the impression from these accounts that the greatest achievement of the Reformation was that it made Higher Criticism possible!

In summarizing the approach of so-called Catholic interpreters of the Articles, one must take care to draw a critical distinction. Some of these (especially those old High Churchmen who wrote before the Ritualist movement) were sharply anti-Roman Catholic and usually careful to exclude a sacerdotalist definition of the ordained ministry. The two best examples here are Bishop William Beveridge (1710) and Bishop Harold Browne (1850).[5] All of this, of course, changed with the publication of John Henry Newman's infamous Tract 90 in 1841. Despite the almost universal condemnation it received at the time, Tract 90 has, in fact, exercised a powerful influence over the years and, as such, it warrants further examination here.

By 1840, the Oxford Movement had come a long way. Its leaders had rightly called Anglicans back to seeing the church as a divine institution, the body of Christ, and not simply a branch of the British civil service. Their advocacy of more frequent communion and attention to better standards both in parish worship and church music were controversial matters in some quarters, but many Evangelicals today would agree that they have merit. The Tracts of the Times that began to appear in 1833 turned up the heat under the simmering controversy and made John Henry Newman truly "the leader of the party."[6] Prior to the appearance of Tract 90, Newman

5. Packer makes this point in *Thirty-Nine Articles,* 37.
6. Neill, *Anglicanism,* 256.

was in an enviable position. At Oxford, he was revered by most students and faculty, and his published sermons had given him a sympathetic following among Anglican clergy throughout the country. Still, Newman remained deeply troubled about the position of the Tractarians within the Church of England. A recent article in the *Dublin Review* by Cardinal Wiseman on the catholicity of the Church of England had rubbed a raw nerve. Newman responded in another periodical but more needed to be said. If Rome had preserved the fullness of the catholic faith better than Anglicanism, was it a serious sin to remain in the Church of England? E. A. Knox aptly describes Newman's predicament this way: "He is anxious to have an answer in controversy why an individual is not bound to leave the English Church, apparently not venturing on anything so bold as a reason why he is bound not to leave it . . . it was to be shown that the Articles were 'patient of a Catholic interpretation,' and free from all taint of heresy."[7]

Newman therefore argued that the Articles did actually teach the "Catholic faith" (or at least they did not explicitly reject it) but that this "Catholic faith" was never really defined with any precision. It was, as E. A. Knox puts it—"a Faith built up by Newman and his friends, and consisting of extracts from the Fathers and the Caroline Divines. Its existence is taken for granted, and the Thirty-Nine Articles are brought into accordance with it, not by what they do say, but always by what they do not say."[8] For instance, regarding Article VI, Newman declared "Holy Scripture is not, on Anglican principles, the rule of Faith." Regarding Article XI: "A number of means go to our justification." Regarding Articles XII and XIII: "Works before Justification do dispose us to receive the grace of God." Regarding Article XXI: "General Councils may err, unless in any case it is promised, as a matter of express supernatural privilege that they shall not err." Regarding Article XXII: This "condemns only the Romish doctrine [of purgatory, pardons, images, invocation of saints]. Others may be held." Regarding Article XXII: "The Article before us neither speaks against the Mass itself, not against its being an offering for the quick and the dead for the remission of sins; but against its being viewed . . . as independent of, or distinct from the sacrifice on the Cross, which is blasphemy."[9]

In summary, then, the argument of Tract 90 involved what Knox terms three major "evasions." First, "the comparison of the Articles with a

---

7. Knox, *Tractarian Movement*, 239, 246.

8. Ibid., 259.

9. Newman quoted in ibid., 261–63, 248.

standard of doctrine which was not in existence, but was an ideal that had to be discovered." A second "evasion" was the ignoring of the great historical fact that "the Articles belonged to an age in which Western Christendom was divided into two great camps, the Roman Catholic and the Protestant, and that the Articles were a declaration that England took her place in the Protestant camp." The final evasion was that Newman contended that the reference in the Declaration to only "the literal and grammatical sense" of the Articles "relieves us from the necessity of making the known opinions of the framers a comment upon the text."[10] This last evasion is perhaps most significant for our purposes here for it effectively detaches the "train" of the Articles from its "engine" (i.e., its original historical context and the original intent of its authors) and essentially allows one to pull Anglicanism anywhere one likes.

Now, some may protest that I am setting up a straw man here just to pulverize it. Tract 90 was, in fact, almost universally condemned and, in the wake of the controversy, publication of the Tracts was suspended and Newman departed for Rome in 1845. Nevertheless, this fanciful, ahistorical approach to the Articles by Anglo-Catholics continued (albeit sometimes in a more subtle form) for decades and has muddied the waters considerably regarding our approach to the Articles. I will use as my example here E. J. Bicknell's *The Thirty-Nine Articles*, a volume that has exercised a broad influence, especially in North America where the standard evangelical works have long been unavailable.

For the authors of the Articles, the heart of the matter was justification. Regarding Article XI, Bicknell contends that it teaches justification by faith but wisely avoids the more "extreme" Reformation teaching on this subject. Bicknell goes on then to explain that the Article does not teach Luther's peculiar understanding: "Luther in his attempt to explain justification spoke of 'an imputed righteousness.' God, he laid down, can treat us as righteous because Christ's righteousness is imputed to us and our sins are imputed to him. This is a 'legal fiction,' and happily our Article, like Scripture, is silent about it. . . . The metaphor expresses a real truth, but is far too external. We cannot put on righteousness like a garment."[11]

This is truly a remarkable assertion, based, as it is, on both an amazing misreading of both Scripture and the clear historical position of the authors of the Articles. Article XI makes explicit reference to the "Homily on

10. Ibid., 259–61.

11. Bicknell, *Theological Introduction*, 206–7.

Justification." Although this Homily does not use the word "imputation" (at least in its positive sense), it clearly describes such a perfect righteousness, external to the believer, which is applied (i.e., imputed) to the believer by God's gracious action in Christ and received through faith alone. The actual word is not there but all that it implies is carefully laid out. Of course, the word itself *was* used by the chief author of the Articles, Thomas Cranmer. In his "Second Sermon on the Creed" from *Catechismus* (1548), Cranmer explains that "by our lively faith in him [i.e., Christ], our sins are forgiven us. . . . For then God no more imputes unto us our former sins; but he imputes and gives unto us the justice and righteousness of his Son Jesus Christ, who suffered for us."[12]

As is often the case, Griffith Thomas furnishes a welcome corrective here. Regarding Article XI, he writes: "This is the great and satisfying doctrine of the imputed righteousness of Christ which is clearly taught by the Article as meritorious on our behalf. It is sometimes argued that this theory is not mentioned in the Article because of its association with what is sometimes called a 'legal fiction.' But in the light of the teaching of the Article on our Lord's merit by which we are accounted righteous before God, the doctrine of imputation is clear, and, indeed, has been taught plainly, as we have just seen, by so representative a man as [Richard] Hooker."[13]

Bicknell provides an equally fanciful reading of Article XXXI. The latter states in disarmingly forthright terms: "the sacrifices of Masses in the which it was commonly said that the priests did offer Christ for the quick and the dead, to have remission of pain or guilt, were blasphemous fables and dangerous deceits." Bicknell stresses that the language here "is most carefully chosen" and then proceeds essentially to gut the original meaning of the Article's authors. He argues that: "There is no denial of the Eucharistic sacrifice, but [only] of popular perversions of it, as embodied in the practical system of worship during the Middle Ages. . . .So it is not 'the sacrifice of the Mass' but the 'sacrifices of masses' that is condemned: not any formal theological statement of the doctrine—for such did not exist—but popular errors."[14]

It is easy to discern Bicknell's sleight of hand here. Again, employing what Newman called "the literal and grammatical sense," he effectively removes the historical context and draws a sophistical distinction without

---

12. Cranmer, in *Writings of the Rev. Dr. Thomas Cranmer*, 173.

13. Thomas, *Principles*, 190.

14. Bicknell, *Theological Introduction*, 417–18.

a difference. (Bicknell is also again following Bishop E. C. S. Gibson's commentary published in 1897.) Griffith Thomas' fifteen-point refutation of this particular interpretation of Article 31 is a *tour de force*. For one, although there was no formal Roman statement of the doctrine in 1553, many earlier statements of it had received some official sanction. Two, Roman Catholic commentators have, in fact, always interpreted this Anglican Article in its plain historical sense as repudiating the official Catholic teaching regarding eucharistic sacrifice! Three, the use of the plural form here is in fact irrelevant, since it was a common expression of the time (employed even by Roman authorities), and was always treated as synonymous with the singular. The connecting "Wherefore" in the Article's wording clearly links the previous part of the Article that "condemns all teaching inconsistent with the uniqueness and completeness of the sacrifice of Christ." Four, the word "altar" was omitted in the Prayer Book of 1552 and never reinserted in subsequent revisions; obviously this fact speaks volumes about the doctrine of eucharistic sacrifice. Five, and perhaps most poignantly, "Cranmer and Ridley died for denying the Roman doctrine of transubstantiation and the Mass; yet this was [like the Forty-Two Articless] before the Council of Trent." In Cranmer's own work on the Lord's Supper, the Archbishop and martyr called the Roman Catholic teaching "that the priests make their Mass a propitiatory sacrifice, to remit the sins as well of themselves as of others, both quick and dead . . . the greatest blasphemy and injury that can be done against Christ."[15] Any repetition of Calvary in the Eucharist was forcefully excluded by all the authors of the Articles; the only sacrifice viewed as a legitimate part of worship in the Holy Communion was the responsive sacrifice of praise and thanksgiving that the faithful communicants offered after receiving the bread and the wine. The whole structure of Cranmer's 1552 rite was designed to underline this truth and no revision up to and including that of 1662 changed this one iota.

Incidentally, Bicknell actually appears here to differ with Newman's mature assessment of this question. In *Via Media* (1883), Newman candidly admitted, "Nothing can come of the suggested distinction between Mass and Masses. . . . What then the 31st Article repudiates is undeniably the central and most sacred doctrine of the Catholic Religion."[16]

Bicknell thus provides ample evidence of how not to interpret the Articles. It remains for me to clarify how one can best approach such a

15. Thomas, *Principles*, 418–19.

16. Newman quoted in Upton, *Churchman's History*, 129–30.

confessional statement. What is the best way to interpret any historical document? Since the 1960s and 70s, several historians of political thought (sometimes called the "Cambridge School") have advocated a "contextualist" approach to historical texts. A student of John Locke, Professor John Dunn, has summarized the method of the Cambridge School as treating "the historical character of the texts as fundamental, and understands these, in the last instance, as highly complex human actions."[17] For these scholars, it is crucial that (to quote another theorist) "the texts are treated in a self-consciously historical manner, through locating them in time and place and, moreover, examining them in their linguistic contexts . . . [the Cambridge School seeks] to introduce a reflexive historical sensitivity to the process of interpretation."[18] Not only is the document's original purpose and historical context crucial to discover and reconstruct but one must attempt to recreate the linguistic context within which particular words or phrases were used. For example, surveying what has been said about liberty from Plato to Mill is rather meaningless unless one is acutely aware of how the meaning of the word "liberty" has shifted and developed over time. The job of an intellectual historian is akin to that of the archaeologist—he attempts to get at the meaning of texts by examining and reconstructing the community of discourse that originally produced a particular text.

What does all this have to do with church confessions? The methodological concerns of intellectual historians should alert us to how naïve and biased Anglicans have been in interpreting our formularies. Both Anglo-Catholics and Evangelicals have been guilty of ahistorical and partisan readings (although because Evangelicals have more often been in sympathy with the central concerns of the Reformers, they have often been fairer interpreters than their High Church opponents). What then would this more thoughtful approach entail for our interpretation of the Articles? Clearly, we must first attempt to reconstruct the communities of discourse that produced the original Forty-Two Articles and its modest Elizabethan revision. We would include in this context the other Reformation formularies such as the Prayer Book (1552), Ordinal and the two Books of Homilies. It would be helpful to also include the extant sermons and letters of the Anglican Reformers (thankfully, we have much of this material reprinted in the Parker Society series and beautifully distilled for us in Philip E. Hughes classic, *The Theology of the English Reformers*). So we do indeed

17. Dunn, "The History of Political Theory," 19.

18. Bell, "The Cambridge School and World Politics." Online. No page numbers.

have the resources at hand to be more accurate, responsible interpreters of the Thirty Nine Articles. But it is hard work that requires the patience of an "archaeologist of ideas."

One valuable historical source that has often been overlooked but which can aid us in what I might term "confessional hermeneutics," is the first complete commentary on the Articles penned by Thomas Rogers. Rogers died in 1616 (we don't know his birth date). He was a graduate of Christ Church, Oxford (BA 1573, MA 1576) and rector of Horningsheath in Suffolk. It is ironic that the commentator favored by Reformed and evangelical churchmen was perhaps most famous during his own time as an opponent of the Puritan Nicholas Bound (d.1613) in the sabbatarian controversy (Rogers believed the sabbatarian teaching of the early Puritans represented a sort of Pharasaical Judaizing and criticized it harshly in several polemical works). Rogers wrote *The English Creede* in 1579 and it was published later in 1607 in a revised form as *The Faith, Doctrine, and Religion professed and protected in the Realm of England and Dominions of the same, expressed in the Thirty-Nine Articles.* When Augustus Toplady set about to prove the Calvinist credentials of the Church of England in 1774 in his book *Historic Proof of the Doctrinal Calvinism of the Church of England*, he highlighted Rogers' commentary. According to Toplady: "There was only one commentary on the Thirty-Nine Articles published in the reign of Queen Elizabeth, that by Thomas Rogers. He dedicated his book to Archbishop Whitgift. In 1607 Rogers dedicated another edition to Archbishop Bancroft. Here is proof that the doctrine of the Church of England is Calvinistic, when the official commentary on the Articles dedicated to two Archbishops of Canterbury and approved by them is thoroughly Calvinistic in tone."[19]

One other source that Toplady mentioned and that is often now neglected is Nowell's *Catechism*. Probably the composition of Alexander Nowell (1507–1602), Dean of St. Paul's, who had been a Marian exile in Strassbourg, it was approved officially by Convocation in 1572. Translated into English from the Latin in 1570 by Thomas Norton and (like Rogers' volume) reprinted by the Parker Society in the 1850s. B. G. Felce refers to the Catechism as "a kind of commentary on the Articles" and, as such, it is an invaluable early source for students of the Articles.[20]

19. Toplady quoted in Felce, "Toplady's View," 35. Toplady once quipped: "Open the liturgy where you will, Calvinism stares you in the face." Ibid., 33.

20. Ibid., 33.

Although he wrote only about a single generation after Cranmer's martyrdom, Thomas Rogers began his commentary on the Articles appropriately by laying out their historical and theological context. In his Preface, he relates the story of Cranmer's correspondence with Calvin regarding a Pan-Protestant meeting to agree on a common doctrinal statement. Sadly, the meeting never materialized but Rogers recounts the exchange in order to stress the unity of doctrine among all the Reformation churches—a "harmony," says Rogers, that "all their confessions doth most sweetly record."[21] Rogers' point here is to lay out the historical and doctrinal context—explain that the Articles should be understood within their Reformation milieu.

Hence one begins to see what an historically-informed interpretation of the Articles might look like. With Rogers and Nowell as our principal guides, often disputed passages become clearer. The contemporary theological context certainly helps elucidate Article XXXI, for example. Rogers' commentary cites in detail and at considerable length those very decrees of Trent that Bicknell and others claim were not actually condemned by the Article. Apparently Rogers was not under any confusion: "It is a fable that the mass is a sacrifice and that propitiatory; a fable, that a few words of a priest can change bread into a living body, yea, many bodies with their souls, and that of Jesus Christ, God and man; a fable, that one and the same sacrifice is offered in the mass which is offered on the cross; a fable, that the said mass is any whit profitable for the quick, much less for the dead."[22]

Now, some may still respond that Article XXXI condemns only an exaggerated medieval understanding of the eucharistic sacrifice. Many since the mid-twentieth century have put forward a more modest conception of the sacrificial character of the Eucharist. The action of the sacrament does not repeat Christ's once for all sacrifice on Calvary's cross but through holy communion worshippers "enter into Christ's self-offering." The sources of this approach are varied (among them Gustav Aulen) and it has had a wide influence: in ecumenical circles as a way to transcend the allegedly arid and unproductive controversies of the Reformation and even among Evangelicals interested in renewing worship (Wheaton worship guru Robert Webber follows this line, for example). John Stott in his superb chapter on the Lord's Supper in *The Cross of Christ* rightly rejects this more refined doctrine of eucharistic sacrifice; I think an application of Article XXXI that interprets it in line with the teaching of its authors must do so also.

21. Rogers, *Catholic Doctrine*, 4.
22. Rogers, *Catholic Doctrine*, 300.

Roger Beckwith, for example, concludes: "The idea that the eucharist is a ritual sacrifice offered by a ministerial priesthood is . . . quite foreign to the New Testament, as is ceremonial suggestive of such an idea; and when the further idea is added that this ritual sacrifice is identical with Christ's sacrifice on the cross, or with some heavenly sacrifice of equal or greater importance, the very foundations of Christianity are being overturned, and the language of Article XXXI, 'blasphemous fables and dangerous deceits,' becomes appropriate."[23]

Yet the current (1979) American BCP teaches such a doctrine implicitly in most of it eucharistic prayers and explicitly in its catechism. The latter describes the Eucharist "is the way by which the sacrifice of Christ is made present, and in which he unites us to his one offering of himself; . . . it is also known as the Divine Liturgy, the Mass, and the Great Offering."

Our troubles with the Articles, however, do not only arise from its Anglo-Catholic interpreters. There are, in fact, at least a couple areas where contemporary Evangelicals may be seriously out of step with the teaching of the Articles. For one, what is our doctrine of the ministry? Most evangelical Anglicans would agree with the classical position of Anglicanism that the Christian ministry is not mediatorial or sacerdotal in nature, but pastoral. Although I am sorry to see the wide acceptance of the title "Father" for Episcopal clergy, I am frankly more concerned these days about evangelical clergy who appear to have adopted a view of the ministry that seems to owe more to the Plymouth Brethren than to Anglicanism. Article XXIII is quite clear about the role and responsibilities of the ordained ministry.

> Of Ministering in the Congregation.
>
> It is not lawful for any man to take upon him the office of public preaching, or ministering the Sacraments in the Congregation, before he be lawfully called, and sent to execute the same. And those we ought to judge lawfully called and sent, which be chosen and called to this work by men who have public authority given unto them in the Congregation, to call and send Ministers into the Lord's vineyard.

Is it not, for instance, contradictory to affirm the Articles and then argue for lay presidency at the Lord's Supper? I am not speaking here about extraordinary circumstances nor about the validity of the sacrament administered by a layman. While all of the Reformers rejected the sacerdotal

---

23. Beckwith, *Thirty-Nine Articles*, 75.

model of the presbyterate, they simultaneously held to a high doctrine of the ministry. This is not clericalism but instead has to do with the proper ordering of the church. Evangelicals have often embraced an egalitarian ethos that owes more to the Enlightenment and democratic individualism than it does to the Bible. I recall chatting with an English evangelical rector who proudly announced that he sat in the congregation during Sunday worship since laymen usually prayed, preached, and led the singing. This is not the position of the Articles nor of Reformed theology in general. Since Evangelicals would be unlikely to argue that very frequent reception of the sacrament was absolutely essential to the Christian faith, can one really make a case for the sort of emergency situation that would require such an extraordinary response as lay administration? I am doubtful that this would be the case, at least in the continental United States.

I suspect that support for lay presidency is also rooted in an unAnglican attitude toward tradition that I see among some evangelical churchmen at present. Of course the English Reformers stressed emphatically the supremacy and sufficiency of Scripture. But at the same time, they recognized a subsidiary role for church tradition, always under and corrected by the word of God but carrying a certain weight. Roger Beckwith again explains helpfully: "The rule that only bishops and presbyters may celebrate communion is . . . extremely ancient. It is not Scripture but tradition, so it is not unalterable. Nevertheless, one does need a good reason to alter it. If traditional customs still serve their original purpose, we should, as Cranmer said, 'have reverence unto them for their antiquity' and not prefer 'innovations and new fangleness.'"[24] When ancient practices are not unscriptural, do they not merit our deference?

Finally, at a time when many Episcopalians are asking about their future within the Episcopal Church, some careful reflection on Article XIX is surely in order. It states:

> Of the Church.
>
> The visible Church of Christ is a congregation of faithful men, in which the pure Word of God is preached, and the Sacraments be duly ministered according to Christ's ordinance, in all those things that of necessity are requisite to the same. As the Church of Jerusalem, Alexandria, and Antioch, have erred, so also the Church of Rome hath erred, not only in their living and manner of Ceremonies, but also in matters of Faith.

24. Beckwith, Latimer Comment, #49, 5.

Since we probably do not need to be reminded about denominations that have erred, direct your attention instead to the first half of this Article. This passage enumerates two marks of the true church, that is, pure doctrine and the sacraments being "duly administered according to Christ's ordinance." Other Protestant Reformers often listed a third mark—biblical discipline. Actually, the Homilies contain a sermon that includes this third mark (a sermon usually attributed to Bishop Jewel), highlighting the importance of "the right use of ecclesiastical discipline." Jewel calls this tripartite definition "agreeable both to the Scriptures of God and also to the doctrine of the ancient Fathers, so that none may justly find fault therewith."[25] Griffith Thomas notes that this third mark may be implied in the word "duly." It is rightly "interpreted," writes Thomas, "to mean all necessary discipline, even to the extent of excommunication of the willfully disobedient."[26]

This sort of discipline has not characterized the Episcopal Church for thirty years or more. What is more disturbing is that many theologically conservative parishes seem to pay little attention to this dimension. They seem to confuse "open communion" which Anglicans practice (unlike Confessional Lutherans, you don't have to have an identical eucharistic theology in order to communicate) with simple indifference. This should not be the case. The teaching of the Articles provides a much-needed corrective here also.

To sum up, an example from juridical theory may be helpful. Legal theorists and politicians have talked a lot about "original intent" in recent years when interpreting the founding "confession" of the American republic; that is, the Federal Constitution of 1787. Note the words of one of its chief architects, James Madison: If "the sense in which the Constitution was accepted and ratified by the Nation . . . be not the guide in expounding it, there can be no security for a consistent and stable government." Or as his friend and neighbor Thomas Jefferson remarked: "Our peculiar security is in the possession of a written constitution. Let us not make it a blank paper by construction [i.e., "interpretation" in modern English]."[27]

Surely much of the dissension within Anglican churches since the mid-nineteenth century is the bitter fruit of not respecting the original intent of

25. Jewel quoted in Thomas, *Principles,* 271–72.

26. Thomas, *Principles,* 242. Rogers was more critical of this approach. See *Catholic Doctrine,* 176–77.

27. Madison and Jefferson quoted by Raoul Berger, *Governed by the Judiciary,* 364.

our framers. When the Anglican formularies become a kind of wax nose that can be shaped by partisans who were avowed enemies of the principles of the English Reformers, then is it any wonder that Anglicanism is in dire straights? As many of us are now involved in the recovery of authentic Anglicanism in North America, let us not shrink from the hard work of understanding the original intent of the Articles and the even harder job of really applying them to the teaching and practice of our congregations.

6

Is the Bible a Book? or, Against Ur-texts

Holy Scripture containeth all things necessary to salvation.

(Article VI)

It is not lawful for the Church to ordain anything that is contrary to God's Word written, neither may it so expound one place of Scripture, that it be repugnant to another.

(Article XX)

Is the Bible—this collection of sixty-six books, many of which are themselves made out of various sources—one book with a meaning? The great effort of the scholarship of the last two hundred years or so has been to get a best text, to understand parts of it better, and to delve behind the text for its origins and *their* meanings. This activity is, of course, extremely interesting and sometimes a new understanding is possible. But it often presupposes or leads to a misconception of what book the Bible is and what authority it has.

New Testament preaching *normally* proclaims the Christ as the fulfillment of Old-Testament prophecy. Jesus himself initiated a tradition when he was thrown out of the synagogue of his home town for saying, of a passage of Isaiah: "This day is this scripture fulfilled in your ears" (Luke 4:21). In St Mark's account, the High Priest rends his clothes and judges that no more evidence of blasphemy is needed when Jesus applies to himself an eschatological prophecy of Daniel: "And behold, one like the Son of man came with the clouds of heaven" (Dan 7:13; Mark 14:62–64). To the two disciples on the road to Emmaus (Luke 24:27): "Beginning at Moses and all the prophets, he expounded unto them in all the Scriptures the things concerning himself." This is a model for subsequent preaching, whether by Peter on the day of Pentecost, Philip, who in answer to the puzzlement of the Ethiopian eunuch, again about Isaiah, "opened his mouth, and began at the same scripture, and preached unto him Jesus" (Acts 8:35), Stephen, or Paul.

So when the message began to be proclaimed beyond the limits of the chosen people, the gentiles had to be given the Old Testament in order to be able to understand the gospel. To this day the missionary endeavor is usually to translate the whole Bible, not just the New Testament.

I dislike Harold Bloom's book *Jesus and Yahweh: The Names Divine*, with its outspoken hatred of the Fourth Gospel, and I think Bloom is just wrong when he says repetitiously things like: "There are no verifiable facts about Jesus of Nazareth," and that there are no reliable reports of either Jesus or his teaching. To say so he has to accuse the author of the Fourth Gospel of direct lying, and Paul of relying on unreliable tradition.[1] But Bloom is certainly on to something when he says: "The New Covenant necessarily founds itself upon a misreading of the Hebrew Bible."[2] The dispute between Christians and Jews is about whether *misreading* is just, but there is common ground that to Christianity one particular reading of the Old Testament is necessary. The fourth-century councils that finalized the canon were continuing the work of Jesus, the understanding of the Scriptures in one particular way, and not the way the Old Testament would be understood as a stand-alone collection. What we call the Old Testament is, then, a very different book from what to the Jews is the Bible, though both works, with some variation about what counts as apocrypha, are exactly the same words in the same order. Bloom's thesis is that both Old and New

---

1. On the reliability of the oral traditions behind the New Testament see: Lyon, *Sign*.

2. Bloom, *Jesus and Yahweh*, 14.

Testaments have been subjected to a process of theologicization resulting in two different Gods. We say, of course, that the same God is revealed in both, but fully by his Son. Where Bloom is right is the observation that the Old Testament on its own makes a sense different from the sense made of it as part of the Christian Bible.

The Christian understanding of Jesus as Messiah, for instance, involves a quite new understanding of Messiahship. The word-root is very common in the Old Testament. In the bit of 1 Samuel I shall mention, the Lord tells Samuel that amongst the sons of Jesse he will find one to be made Messiah, that is, anointed king. Jews point out quite reasonably that, as far as we know, Jesus was never anointed, except by the woman who was a sinner and anointed his feet (Luke 7:38), nor did he ever claim to be king of Israel in anything like the same way as Saul or David or Solomon.

So: Does the Old Testament actually mean what the New Testament writers say it does? When Jesus expounds "the things concerning himself," do they really and truly concern himself? My contention is that this, which I think is the right question, will not be answered by Old Testament scholarship, but by the authority of revelation shown in the coherence of a whole book; and it is to be answered by faith, under the guidance of the Holy Spirit. But faith is not the enemy of intelligence. If the full and proper reading of the Bible is not quite the same as the full and proper reading of either a poem, a history, the account of an experiment, or a mathematical equation, the philosophically interesting thing is that it must be reasonable to recognize this special case and unreasonable to deny it. In any case we are thinking about a *reading* not a decoding of something cryptic.

The common notion of prophecy in our world is not quite the same as the one practiced by the children of Israel. The Jewish canon, unlike the Christian, was not finalized by any synod or council. One rabbinic explanation of why some authentic-looking prophecies did not make their way in is that, "Many prophets arose in Israel . . . but only a prophecy which had validity for generations (*viz.* did not only pertain to specific historical circumstances) was written (*viz.* was included in the biblical corpus); a prophecy which did not have validity for generations was not written (included)."[3] As Mr. Anthony Weston says,

> The Bible does not use the word "fulfillment" (*pleroma*) entirely in accordance with contemporary usage. When, for example, Matthew's Gospel quotes Hosea xi, "Out of Egypt I have called my

3. Talmon, "The Crystallisation of the 'Canon of Hebrew Scriptures,'" 10.

son," it says that these words were "fulfilled" in the experience of Christ. This expression means that Matthew sees a cogent and instructive parallel. Readers (especially his Jewish readers) would be fully conscious that [originally this passage referred to] the people of Israel. Matthew is not arguing and is not understood to be arguing that the "fulfillment" of this prophecy was an example of divine foreknowledge to substantiate the Messianic status of Jesus Christ.[4]

Prophecy is incomplete without application, and the prophecy cannot itself decide whether the application is valid, nor even whether it is a prophecy. Jesus on the cross prayed Psalm 22, and St John applies it to the casting of lots for his garments (John 19:24). This use of the Psalm is a fulfillment of prophecy in what was an accustomed way, the praying in one situation of a hymn written for another, or for all. The Psalm was never so fully itself as at that moment, though we can go on praying it. The Suffering Servant passages of Isaiah can be applied only with difficulty and ingenuity to what is known of the politics contemporary with him. How could they have been understood at the time? They come into their own in the New Testament. Such is prophecy!

The treatment of Scripture as prophetic was not confined to the prophetic books. The Psalms, as we saw, could be prophetic, and even an event in the Book of Numbers could be taken as a type. It would be unintelligible to take the account of the brazen serpent (Num 21:7–10) as deliberately *referring forward* to the crucifixion of our Lord. But it is very intelligible— Christians would say, convincing—to see in it a type or foreshadowing which could not have been recognized as such before the latter event.

The New Testament is written in Greek, and quotes the Hebrew Scriptures in Greek; a language to which the modern notion of the fulfillment of prophecy, that is, prediction verified, comes more naturally. The first relevant difference is that, believe it or not if you know no Hebrew, Old Testament Hebrew has no tenses. It does have two basic forms of the verb which grammarians often misleadingly call tenses—misleadingly, for how can a "tense" be called imperfect or future at the discretion of the grammarian? The distinction is between finished and ongoing actions, but both may occur in past, present, or future. Perfective aspect is ordinarily expressed in English only by the perfect tense, which can be misleading.

Some Old Testament prophecy does of course refer to the future, even the near future, as when Elisha predicts that, "Tomorrow about this time

---

4. Weston, *Apologia pro Fide Mea*, 3 (unpublished).

shall a measure of fine flour be sold for a shekel" (2 Kgs 7:1). (The Hebrew here does not use a verb at all!) But if the whole language is really tenseless, it is natural to take many utterances as timeless, a sort of present eternally useable in new situations, in the way we have just glanced at. When I was in charge of the parish nine-lessons-and-carols service a few of years ago, I tried the experiment of removing all future tenses from the Old Testament passages and it worked surprisingly well! ("Behold, a virgin conceives and bears a son," etc.) It may have been a help that the primitive tense structure of English (in Old English there are only two tenses, present and past) still survives in places, so that a present tense can have a future sense, as in "I return to England next week." But the nearest thing I can think of to the Hebrew habit in a tensed language is the way we report the action of plays or novels. In *Pride and Prejudice,* Lydia runs away with Wickham. It is not quite correct in such cases to use the preterite (ran away) and the future would be just wrong. The action does take place with a beginning a middle and an end, but in a kind of eternal present.

Hebrew grammatical forms not found in English include *intensive* and *causative* forms of the verb, so that when Samuel hews Agag to pieces before the Lord in Gilgal, the word that the 1611 Bible translated as *hewed* is not found elsewhere in the Old Testament, and is variously translated, but the one thing the scholars are sure of is that it is a *piel* form, so whatever Samuel did he did it very much or very intensely. Hebrew has *katal,* he kills, but also *kitel* he very much kills, and *hiktil* he causes to kill. When the Psalmist prays, "Cause thy face to shine, O Lord" we can be sure that the Hebrew behind our rather odd verbal phrase "cause to shine" is a simple one-word *hiphil* form, meaning, "cause to do so-and-so."

These all make for awkwardness of translation. With tenses, the habit of the Indo-European languages makes a translation easier to a Christian reading. The New Testament, written in a language with just about all imaginable tenses, pluperfect, future perfect, etc., is a more natural home than Biblical Hebrew for the idea of once-for-all temporal fulfillment of prophecy. It is undeniable that the New Testament does, frequently, *fix* a prophecy and identify it with one particular moment, in a way that comes far more naturally to Greek than to Hebrew.

So: is the New Testament what Bloom calls it, the "strongest and most successful misreading in all of textual history"?[5] I don't think so. The whole

---

5. Bloom, *Jesus and Yahweh,* 36.

New Testament gloss on the Old is neither arbitrary nor unreasonable, though it could not be predicted from the Old Testament.

When a commentator tells us that: "We are indebted to [Joel] for immortal language about the outpouring of the Spirit, even though we may not be able to go so far as to say that he is the prophet of Pentecost,"[6] he directly contradicts the oldest Christian sermon, when on the Day of Pentecost Peter proclaimed: "This is that which was spoken by the prophet Joel" (Acts 2:16). The commentator misunderstands prophecy in a way that prevents the Bible from delivering the gospel. Peter is seeing a fulfillment of prophecy in a traditional way but also fixing the fulfillment to this one event.

He that seeketh, findeth. The claim is not that the common reader, opening the book at the beginning of Genesis and closing it at the end of Revelation, would be expected to be converted to Christ, though that is not impossible. The common reader will bring with him presuppositions (which will vary with, amongst other things, time and place), about what is likely and unlikely, possible and impossible, good and bad. Evelyn Waugh's story gives Randolph Churchill's response to the Old Testament as that of a common reader, and not necessarily a bad one. "Thinking the money well spent if it would keep Randolph quiet, Freddy and I have bet him £10 each that he will not read the Bible right through in a fortnight. He has set to work but not as quietly as we hoped. He sits bouncing about on his chair, chortling and saying, 'I say, did you know this came in the Bible "bring down my grey hairs with sorrow to the grave"?' Or simply, 'God, isn't God a shit.'"[7] The reader of Holy Scripture needs to be like the Ethiopian eunuch, a seeker after truth, guided by the Holy Spirit usually with the help of the church. (It is noticeable that those who believe in *sola scriptura* are generally the authors of the longest sermons: Scripture is alone but needs expounding.) Nevertheless, the Christian sense of the Bible is not fixed arbitrarily. Once it is grasped, the Christian reading is seen to be truly that of the whole collection of such disparate writings, which it would be unreasonable to deny.

This is not to claim that all Christian understandings are easy. To mention just an obvious example, the interpretation of Psalm 110, used by Jesus himself and at three later places in the New Testament, would not convince any ordinary literary critic. The Gospel according to St. Matthew

6. Brown, "Joel," 564.

7. Davie, *Diaries of Evelyn Waugh,* 591.

reports Jesus asking the question if the Christ is the son of David: "How then doth David in spirit call him Lord, saying 'The Lord said unto my Lord, Sit thou at my right hand, until I make thine enemies thy footstool'? If David then calls him Lord, how is he his son?" (Matt 22:42–45). The Hebrew here uses the two different words both translated *Lord*, which the 1611 Bible distinguishes typographically. The divine name is given small caps but is traditionally read aloud as the same word as the second *Lord*, Adonai, so in reading aloud the same word would be used twice. The first, however, represents the tetragrammaton, the name of God which must not be taken in vain, the second the word for an ordinary earthly lord. (God can, of course, be both, as in the opening words of Psalm 8, translated "O LORD our Lord" in 1611, but "O Lord our Governor" by Coverdale.) It is hard not to take the Psalm as meaning that the Lord God of Israel speaks to an earthly (though anointed) Lord, the King of Israel, saying "Sit thou on my right hand," and that the Psalmist here is either not David or David speaking of himself like Caesar or de Gaulle in the third person. (It is quite possible that Jesus here was citing the Greek of the Septuagint not the original Hebrew. The Greek like the English just repeats *kurios*, Lord, though the Hebrew uses the two words as I have reported.)

Or consider the text at the center of much controversy for nearly two thousand years: "Behold, a virgin shall conceive, and bear a son" (Isa 7:14), one of the prophetic texts used from the beginnings of Christianity and as late as Handel's *Messiah*, uses the word *almah* meaning (according to the Brown-Driver-Briggs Hebrew and English Lexicon) "young woman (ripe sexually, maid or newly married)," but with no definite sense of virginity. The Septuagint thought it *did* mean *virgin* and translated *parthenos*, and again, New Testament dependence on Greek rather than Hebrew is possible. (A later Greek translation uses *neanis* [youth] because, it is suggested, the Jews wanted to make Christian misinterpretation impossible.) By the way I don't know why the 1611 Bible uses the indefinite article "a" (not found in Hebrew), because the Hebrew uses a definite article, *the* virgin (or the young woman), as does the Greek. However we understand *almah*, the application to Blessed Mary, is a rather extreme example of the fulfillment of prophecy, for throughout the prophetic writings Israel and Judah are constantly personified as young women, and it seems more natural to take Isaiah in that sense. Nevertheless, to take the birth of our Lord as a fulfillment of this prophecy is not an impossible reading.

A graver problem for me is the doctrine of the above quoted Article, that (to paraphrase) if the Bible is one book it must not contradict itself. The New Testament is in fact very selective. Esther is not much cited, thank goodness! But is it possible without contradicting the Articles of Religion to say that the whole story of the conquest of the Promised Land by the Israelites is based on a wrong understanding of the will of God? The conquest is the sign that they are the chosen people. But if so an essential early chapter of the whole developing revelation is divinely commanded genocide. The fall of Jericho is a model. "And they utterly destroyed all that was in the city, both man and woman, young and old, and ox, and sheep, and ass, with the edge of the sword" (Josh 6:21). The Psalm rather harps on the fate of Og king of Bashan: "And slew famous kings: for his mercy endureth for ever / Sihon king of the Amorites: for his mercy endureth for ever / and Og the king of Bashan: for his mercy endureth for ever" (Ps 136:18–20), without suggesting that he had done anything worse to deserve his fate than defend his people against the aggression of Israel. Samuel pronounces the deposition of the first anointed king of Israel because he has failed to "go and utterly destroy the sinners the Amalekites, and fight against them until they be consumed" and then in person, as we saw: "Samuel [extremely] hewed Agag in pieces before the LORD in Gilgal" (1 Sam 15:18–33). Must a Christian really believe that Samuel is there obedient to God?

I have no answer to the problem of the parts of the Old Testament apparently unsusceptible to Christian reading, which as a literary critic I have to acknowledge without playing down. But I do say, as a reader and critic, that the problem is not serious enough to destroy the substantial unity of the Bible when the Bible is read in a right spirit.

The classical Lutheran conception of the unity and authority of Scripture, as far as I understand it, is better *as literary criticism* than the position of the Humanists (below), as far as I understand *that*. Work of great interest to ordinary literary critics was done by theologians driven by the necessity of understanding how the Bible is one book. How are works of art wholes? How, for instance, can the end of a play be said to affect the beginning within a whole? Gadamer reports that: "All the details of a text were to be understood from the *contextus* and the *scopus*, the unified sense at which the whole aims." The sense of the parts which make the whole is itself modified by the whole.[8] Gadamer is mistaken when he sees a contradiction in this position: "By ultimately asserting the Protestant credal formulae

---

8. Gadamer, *Truth and Method*, 177.

as guides to the understanding of the unity of the Bible, it too supersedes the scriptural principle in favor of a rather brief Reformation tradition."[9] Whether this applies to Lutheranism I don't know (Luther himself was notoriously rude about the Epistle of James, but it remains in the canon), but I think the Church of England can plead not guilty. The three classical creeds are common ground to Romans and Protestants. They do offer to sum up the teaching of Scripture, but Scripture remains the court of appeal. If it were somehow shown that something in a creed was unsupported by or contrary to Scripture it would be the creed that would have to change, not Scripture. That the situation does not arise shows that the creeds in fact accurately summarize the Bible.

If the Bible is one book we have a remarkable demonstration that, to put it mildly, there is more than one way of making a book a unity. (I can only think of one example in imaginative literature of how an addition can make a different sense of what is added to. When Jean de Meun completed *The Romance of the Rose* by adding a long section to what Guillaume de Lorris had left unfinished at his death, the second part cast an ironic light back on the first and gave a different understanding of the whole.) Well, that is the older way of looking at it, displaced now by the various forms of criticism, high, low, and deconstructionist.

The improvement of our understanding of the text is fine as long as it takes place within the context of the Bible. It is usually of small details. For example, in 1 Samuel 13:2, occurs a word which nobody, Christian nor Jew, understood, the noun *pim*, so the translators had a stab at making what sense they could. The passage reports how the Philistines took measures to prevent the Israelites from preparing possibly offensive weapons; but they *were* allowed (in the 1611 translation) "a file for the mattocks and for the coulters and for the forks and for the axes, and to sharpen the goads." (I don't know without a dictionary what a mattock is.) It now turns out, thanks to the twentieth-century archaeological discovery of ancient weights marked *pim*, uniformly two thirds of a shekel, that a *pim* was not a file, but the measure of what the Israelites had to pay the Philistines. The word translated *forks* in the same passage is another measure, one third of a shekel, but rendered *tridentum* by Jerome, with which later translators made do until the archaeological discovery. All well and good.

But what if modern scholarship gives us genuine advances about the original texts of a kind that if accepted alter the whole book? I give an

9. Ibid., 177.

example of work in progress by a distinguished scholar whose friend I have the honor to be.

Professor David Wulstan thinks that the Masoretic text of the whole Book of Psalms is radically corrupt, that somewhere along the line there has been a break in oral transmission, and that the verses of the Psalms were originally on the whole much shorter, and in some sort of regular accentual meter, not just the rhythmical prose with rhetorical elements like parallelisms, end-cola cadences, pausal forms, etc. such as we have in the present text, and in the translations of the LXX and Jerome (and Coverdale). Wulstan produces numbers of examples of different kinds of corruption (Northern forms, deliberate archaisms, change of pronunciation of disyllables to make them trisyllables, survival of desinentials but misunderstood and mispronounced, etc.) some of which are incontrovertible. For instance, if the verses originally had a regular number of syllables, it would immediately upset the meter when Adonai began to be substituted for the divine Name, because Adonai has an extra syllable.

Now, whether Wulstan is right I am not equipped to judge, and whether he can get as far as conjectural emendations *metri causa* that will persuade other learned scholars I do not know. My question is whether, in the quite imaginable case that an important biblical text could be radically changed by the efforts of the scholars, or by a new Qumran cave with texts radically different from ours, this would affect the Bible. To this, against scholarly consensus, the answer is *no*.

The text of the Bible is not like the text of a poet. If Shakespeare's foul papers turned up it is certain that a number of textual cruces would be solved and the plays read and performed accordingly. If there were some almost unimaginable discovery of original texts of some psalms guaranteed to be composed by King David, and preferably with musical notation, they would certainly be very different from what is offered up in praise daily by the whole church. But the Psalms are as our Lord prayed them, and as we pray them and shall go on praying them whatever textual discoveries are made. The later, arguably corrupt text of the Psalms, is part of the Bible, and has been blessed by God in the church's use of it. The word of God written is not an ur-text in principle determinable by scholars.

Professor Wulstan himself has coined the useful word *accurantism* as the antonym of *obscurantism*. The latter word, which seems to be a translation of a term coined by Reuchlin, has been very useful in the history of the scholarly take-over of the text. Erasmus' editions of the Greek New

Testament are, of course, of profound importance in the history of Christendom. But from Erasmus to the position that the text is always subject to restoration, emendation, and improvement, is a step much encouraged if opponents can be labeled *obscurantist*, which is one of those useful words like *racist* and *sexist* that put an end to reasoned discussion. It is not unreasonable, however, to hold the opinion that the New Testament as an authoritative interpretation of the Old makes a coherent book that ceases to be coherent if the Old Testament texts are radically altered, which, of course, doesn't prevent work on the text being, as I said, fascinating.

A fortiori our use of the Bible is unaffected by source-studies. Scholars have long searched for the sources of Shakespeare, but the plays are what he made of them. The Bible is what numerous authors and editors, Jesus, the apostles, and the church made of sources, guided by the Holy Ghost.

Some notion of *textus receptus* is necessary to the unity of the Holy Scriptures. When this is not understood there are bad effects on translation. The translator of the Bible should be trying to give as exact as possible an imitation in the "target" language of as near as he can get to the best text approved by the fourth-century councils. Then he can add what he knows about changed understandings, sources, etc., in the textual apparatus. By all means let there be notes explaining these things, but preferably prefaced by the kind of argument I am offering to explain why the biblical text is unaltered. The *almah* of Isaiah 7:14 should be translated *virgin* because that is how the word is understood in the Christian Bible. When Matthew uses the text as a proof-quotation, the Good News Bible (in North America called *Today's English Version*) translates it as: "A virgin will become pregnant and have a son" (Matt 1:23). But the same version translates the text in the Old Testament, Isaiah 7:14, as "A young woman who is pregnant will have a son." This makes Matthew misquote. It is dissection not translation, because the translators were mistaken about what it was that they were trying to translate.

Inspiration is a concept that needs some development. If there were original authors (somewhere in Babylonia?) a long way behind the myths of Genesis 1, were *they* inspired? Was the Deuteronomist reviser of the earlier Torah inspired? (Jesus certainly thought so.) The evangelist who put together different sources, themselves edited, in the first Gospel, was inspired just as were the edited sources. The Fourth Gospel revising and filling in the record of the Synoptics was inspired. Paul, and then Peter and James commenting on Paul, were all inspired. Canon-formation is part of the process of making the one Book. If inspiration is a continuous process, the church can have been inspired as well as the writers and the editors. The councils were inspired in confirming as the canon what for the most part was already common knowledge. The councils concluded the work of Jesus of understanding the Scriptures in one particular way. Translators too can be inspired to make a book acceptable as the Bible.

If we are bold enough to resist accurantism it may be seen that even mistranslation can be inspired. The role of scholarship is not to alter the word of God written, but to elucidate and annotate it. By all means let them tell us that our Lord misunderstood Psalm 110. But his [mis]understanding of it is that of the Bible. It is the Bible, the book made in the early Christian centuries, that is the word of God written, and the book to be translated. When the Bible is allowed to be itself it does indeed tell, as the Sunday-school hymn used to put it, the old, old story that Christ Jesus makes thee whole.

7

Gregory Dix and the Reformation Liturgy

BRYAN D. SPINKS

Paul Bradshaw wrote: "Of all Anglican liturgical scholars, Gregory Dix (1901–1952) is unquestionably the one who has exercised the greatest influence not only within the Anglican Communion but also outside it."[1] Even though this book included short biographies of such distinguished liturgical scholars as F. E. Brightman, A. G. Hebert, Pearcy Dearmer, Edward Ratcliff, and Massey Shepherd, Bradshaw's remark is undoubtedly correct. Much of Dix's fame, of course, rests with his work *The Shape of the Liturgy*. He certainly published works on other liturgical material, notably baptism and confirmation, ordination, and reservation of the sacrament, as well as on other topics. However, none of these received the attention that *The Shape* did, and none have been anywhere near as influential. The fact that the book is still in print is a testimony to its success, even though many students and clergy who read it are probably unaware of just how much of it is now out of date to the point of being seriously misleading. One of its greatest appeals is its readability—"like a novel, but is in fact a serious contribution to scholarship" was a remark that Edward Ratcliff is reputed to have made.[2] More recent reflections on Dix by Simon Bailey and Simon

1. Bradshaw, "Gregory Dix," 111.
2. Stevenson, *Gregory Dix—Twenty-Five Years On*, 38.

Jones have reminded us of the human side of this "Anglo-Papalist," and both his pastoral abilities and his vocation as a monk.[3] Something of the many sides to Dix was captured by John Rawlinson, Bishop of Derby, in the obituary which appeared in The Times: "By the death of Gregory Dix the Church of England has lost one of her most gifted and distinguished sons. A historian and scholar of no mean order, he had also a highly original cast of mind (reflected in his massive and learned *Shape of the Liturgy*)—qualities which, together with an impish sense of humour and a streak of sheer naughtiness, made his company a constant delight to those who were fortunate enough to be his friends. He was a superb raconteur and an extremely lovable man."[4]

Yet like most of us, Dix had blind spots, and one of the most glaring was noted by Kenneth Stevenson: "His overt lack of sympathy with the reformation shows up one of his greatest limitations."[5] This paper explores some of Dix's ideas on Christian initiation and the Eucharist, as well as his beliefs about the so-called *Apostolic Tradition* of Hippolytus, in relation to this blind spot or prejudice against the Reformation and Cranmer's liturgical compilations.

1. The Apostolic Tradition

One of the greatest influences on twentieth-century liturgical revision was the "discovery" and subsequent publication of the document called *Apostolic Tradition* attributed to Hippolytus of Rome, and dated c. 215. The text was isolated at the beginning of the twentieth century by Schwarz and Connolly. It was Dom Bernard Botte who made it famous in the Roman Catholic Church with his French edition of 1963, but it was Dix who made it famous years before in England with his edition in 1937. It was regarded as being the indisputable pure Western rite of the third century, and amongst scholars and practitioners alike it came to be regarded as self-evidently the liturgy that all should aspire to and adopt to get behind the Reformation disputes and find ecumenical agreement. Scholarship at the end of the twentieth century has questioned the authenticity of the document. The statue found in Rome, the plinth of which listed works, some of which were

3. Bailey, *A Tactful God: Gregory Dix Priest, Monk and Scholar*; Jones, *The Sacramental Life: Gregory Dix and His Writings*.

4. Jones, *Sacramental Life*, xx–xxi.

5. Stevenson, *Gregory Dix—Twenty-Five Years On*, 37.

by Hippolytus, and which was restored with a man's head, is now thought by many to have been of a woman signifying wisdom. Allen Brent argued strongly and convincingly that the "Hippolytus corpus" was the collection and preserved memories of a dissident house church in Rome.[6] Furthermore, there is little justification for calling the work, isolated and recovered from a number of church orders, like a liturgical "Q," "Apostolic Tradition." Finally, the isolated document seems to be a compilation of sources, and while Stewart-Sykes wishes to preserve a mid-third century date for the compilation, Bradshaw, Johnson, and Philips suggest a fourth century date, and a compilation that expressed an imagined "golden age" of the past.[7] In other words, rather than having Roman use of 215 AD, the document is a compilation looking back and recreating an imagined golden past.

That was not the case in Dix's day, though, and he expended a great deal of time and scholarship expounding this document and commending it as ancient use. So he could write, "It represents the mind and practice not of St. Hippolytus only but of the whole Catholic Church of the second century. As such it is of outstanding importance."[8] Implicit at a subliminal level was the idea that what Catholics did in the second century was what should be done now. The influence of the document has been immense in both the liturgical reforms of Vatican II and in the Anglican Communion. Had the Eucharistic Prayer of Addai and Mari had the same influence, it could be reasonably argued that this ancient Semitic prayer has been in continuous use from probably the end of the third century, and is authentic. With the so-called *Apostolic Tradition*, in hindsight we might ask why any church would want to adopt for its normal Sunday Eucharistic prayer an idealized Eucharistic Prayer from a fourth century dissident group, put forward for use at an Ordination of a bishop rather than a normal Sunday Eucharist? It warns against investing too heavily in scholarly findings and fads.

2. Initiation

Dix's two major contributions to the debate on initiation in Anglicanism were *Confirmation or the Laying on of Hands?* (1936) and *The Theology of Confirmation in relation to Baptism* (1946). As an Anglo-Catholic of the

6. Brent, *Hippolytus and the Roman Church.*

7. Hippolytus. *On the Apostolic Tradition*; Bradshaw et.al., *Apostolic Tradition: A Commentary.*

8. Dix, *Treatise on the Apostolic Tradition of St. Hippolytus of Rome*, xliv.

"Anglo-Papalist" type, Dix was committed to the then Roman Catholic position that Confirmation was a sacrament, and that it was a sacrament administered by the bishop. In recent years Rome has reiterated the sacramental status of Confirmation as a rite that confers the Spirit, but has allowed its delegation to presbyters. However, central to Anglo-Catholic belief was the importance of the Episcopal office (even if individual bishops had to be disobeyed), and maintenance of the medieval Western and Tridentine definition of seven sacraments.

As a liturgical scholar, Dix chose to apply his doctrinal commitments to the liturgical evidence, which included an appeal to the New Testament. In his 1936 work Dix argued that Baptism was a preliminary to Confirmation, and the latter was the Christian equivalent to circumcision. He found references to Confirmation in the New Testament, and the Apostolic Fathers, arguing that the term "Seal" was the same as Confirmation, and was originally an anointing with oil. His 1946 work followed on the controversy aroused by the 1944 Report *Confirmation Today*, which, using the Book of Common Prayer texts on a *lex orandi, lex credendi* mode, stated that the Spirit was given in Baptism, and in Confirmation there was a further outpouring of divine power completing what had been done in Baptism. The view in the report was criticized by Dr. L. S. Thornton CR and Bishop Kenneth Kirk, though the latter seems to have argued from the text of the Roman Confirmation prayer rather than that of the Church of England rite. A. M .Ramsey replied to Bishop Kirk, arguing that if in Baptism we are in Christ, then being in Christ means having the Spirit.[9] Dix argued that whereas Baptism removed original sin, it was Confirmation that gave the Spirit and completed Baptism. However, Dix argued from history—and in this case from the authority of the so-called *Apostolic Tradition*. First, he argued that since practice preceded scriptural canon, the *parodosis* of practice is as important. Thus he wrote: "The fullest early account of the liturgy of initiation is that contained in the *Apostolic Tradition* of St. Hippolytus, a document compiled, as its title suggests, as a record of this authoritative *paradosis* of practice at the time when its authority was first beginning to be disregarded. In its details this represents the practice at Rome in the later second century."[10]

---

9. For a summary and bibliographic details see: Fisher, *Confirmation Then and Now*, 145–48.

10. Dix, *Theology of Confirmation in Relation to Baptism*, 10.

Dix went on to argue that Baptism in the fathers always meant more than simply the ritual washing in water; it always included other things. He named Pseudo-Eusebius of Emesa as a major source of the (mis)understanding that the Holy Spirit was conferred in the water ritual, and confirmation was simply an increase of grace, and it was bequeathed to the medieval church via the False Decretals. Turning to the 1552 rite of Confirmation, Dix asked: "Is it too much to see in this 'daily increase,' compared with the 'Form' of 1549, the final triumph in England of Pseudo-Eusebius over that primitive Apostolic Tradition of the liturgy which had hitherto managed to preserve itself intact in practice right down through the Middle Ages from the very earliest days of the Church?"[11]

Although Dix was motivated by older liturgical tradition, his theological position was only tenable if Confirmation followed immediately after Baptism, which was indeed one of the suggestions that followed on the 1944 report. However, what is noteworthy is that Dix appealed from his doctrinal presuppositions to the ancient texts, and the Prayer Book texts themselves were shunted into a siding.

Whether he would have approved of the redrafting that was in the 1980 Alternative Service Book or the Common Worship 2000 texts is of course an interesting and futile question. We may assume that given the then Roman practice of holding First Communion after First Confession rather than after Confirmation, he may not have objected to the growing practice in some Anglican provinces of admitting baptized children to communion. On the other hand, in the 1946 work he emphasized that the problem *per se* was not Confirmation, but infant baptism, and that could be administered providing it was regarded "as an abnormality, wholly incomplete by itself and absolutely needing completion by the gift of the Spirit and the conscious response of faith for the full living of the Christian 'eternal life' in time."[12]

What is important, though, is the manner in which he read back into the New Testament and the selected liturgies his own doctrinal beliefs. Very few scholars would today accept Dix's interpretation of the New Testament texts, and few liturgical scholars would view the diversity of the pre-Nicene period as all supporting the interpretation Dix wished to give. In fact, the detachment of Confirmation as a separate rite was a Western development, and has no counterpart in the ancient Eastern rites. The reservation of the

11. Ibid., 29.
12. Ibid., 31.

rite to bishops reflected the practice of Rome, and may have arisen as a reiteration of the presbyteral anointing when a monarchical bishop was established, or as some Episcopal jurisdiction over differing ethnic and linguistic ecclesial groups in Rome. Thomas Cranmer's understanding and use of Confirmation is more complex, but to preserve the rite for adults making a profession of faith, as a non-identical repetition or reiteration of Baptism, is certainly one legitimate pastoral use of the rite, without necessarily investing it with the theology presupposed by Dix.[13]

3. The Eucharist

A number of Dix's writings impinged on the Eucharist, both doctrine and liturgy, but by far the most important was *The Shape of the Liturgy*. There he argued that later forms were less important than the underlying structure of the Eucharist: "What was fixed and immutable everywhere in the second century was the outline or Shape of the Liturgy, what was *done*. What our Lord instituted was not a 'service,' something said, but an action, something done—or rather the continuance of a traditional Jewish action, but with a new meaning, to which he attached a consequence. The new meaning was that henceforward this action was to be done 'for the *anamnesis* of Me'; the consequence was that 'This is My Body' and 'The cup is the New Covenant in My Blood.'"[14]

As is well known, Dix argued that a seven-action shape at the Last Supper was everywhere reproduced as a four-action shape—taking, thanksgiving, breaking, and communion. Dix's evidence for the offertory was in some cases a misreading of the evidence, and as subsequent studies have attempted to show (but the popularity of Dix overshadows these), there were two main actions, Thanksgiving and Communion, and two utilitarian actions which only subsequently became ritualized with texts and explanation—the presentation of the bread and wine, and the breaking of the bread.[15] Dix also built on his own readings and interpretations of some of the patristic liturgical text—particularly Serapion—but happily assumed his suggestions had become assured facts of scholarship. This four-action shape, so useful in Anglican confirmation classes, has become Dix's

13. Spinks, "Cranmer, Baptism and Christian Nurture," 98–110.

14. Dix, *Shape*, 214–15.

15. Michell, *Landmarks in Liturgy*; Buchanan, *End of the Offertory*; Spinks, "Mis-Shapen: Gregory Dix and the Four Action Shape of the Liturgy," 161–77.

hallmark, even though, consciously or unconsciously, he was only rediscovering what a number of sixteenth- and seventeenth-century divines had taught.[16] The difference was that Dix believed that the Book of Common Prayer had departed from the clarity of this four-action shape, whereas his Anglican precursors found it quite clearly expressed in the Book of Common Prayer. Part of the difference is to be explained by Dix's own dislike of the Reformation and the Cranmerian liturgy.

The Shape was and remains an interesting piece of scholarship in which Dix discussed and presented a great deal of early and patristic liturgical texts upon which to build his case for the underlying shape, and the fact that the Eucharist was a ritual action rather than texts. His discussion of the evolution of the Eucharist, and particularly of the Western rite, led him to speak of strata, with primary, and secondary strata being finally overlaid with tertiary devotional strata of medieval piety. He indicated a development from "doing" to "seeing" and "hearing" Mass, and then an individualism which was concerned with "thinking" and "feeling." The logic would be to remove the external action altogether and so leave the individual's mental appreciations of and reactions to the passion and the atonement in complete possession of the field.[17] Quakers had taken this path, but Dix felt that Protestants were stuck mid-way. The Book of Common Prayer communion service thus was defective in shape, since it had departed from the primitive shape, and defective in focus, since it concentrated on medieval personal contemplation of the atonement. For many this seemed a sound enough argument. However, Dix, as a monk of Nashdom, used the then current Roman Mass, which certainly had many of those tertiary elements he was critical of, and much of the piety surrounding the Roman Mass was as focused on the passion and atonement as any Protestant devotion was. Somehow Dix's Anglo-Papalism prevented him from seeing the contradiction. More importantly, though, it must be questioned whether Dix's accusations against the Reformation rites were valid.

Like Dix himself and all of us, Cranmer was a man of his age—he could not have been other. He certainly did have some knowledge of liturgy—probably as much an authority in the sixteenth century as Dix was in the twentieth. Cranmer knew some of the Eastern rites, but on the whole did not use them. He had access to a Visigothic text, which he used in his baptismal rite of 1549, and some of it was retained in 1552. He also drew

16. Spinks, *Two Faces of Elizabethan Anglican Theology.*

17. Dix, *Shape,* 600.

on contemporary material, Catholic and Protestant. He knew the patristic writings as well as most of his peers, and also knew much of the "new theology" which came from Germany and Switzerland. He framed a rite which in its 1552 form, when that of 1549 was now "faithfully and godly pursued, explained and made fully perfect" expressed what he regarded as a biblical concept of sacrifice—ourselves, our souls and bodies, along with prayer, praise and almsgiving—with an expression of justification by faith. He believed that the rite was drawing on the best of the past, and that he was restoring the rite to an earlier purity.

H. O. Old has shown that many of the reformed theologians believed their liturgies expressed what they read in the fathers.[18] We may now think that they were wrong, but their reading of their present agenda into the fathers was no worse than Dix reading his agenda into patristic liturgy. However, Dix pressed his case by identifying Cranmer as a Zwinglian, with the *a priori* understanding that no informed Christian would wish to be a Zwinglian. This labeling was a subtle way of conviction of a crime before the trial. Zwingli's position was one that, apart from Oecolampadius and the early Bullinger, no Reformer endorsed without considerable qualification, and the Reformed Confessions clearly regarded Zwingli's position as inadequate. Dix remained silent on this. His treatment of Calvin was limited to the 1559 Institutes, though omitting the passage where Calvin states that the worthy communicant receives the substance of the body and blood of Christ. His treatment of these Reformers is quite at variance with the depth and breadth of his concern for the early liturgical material. Dix did enter the debate over whether Cranmer was a "Zwinglian" or a "Calvinist." More recent scholarship has tended to acknowledge that Cranmer's Eucharistic doctrine was of a Swiss flavor but has tended to class it as "Cranmerian."[19] Furthermore, subsequent Church of England divines, and not just the Durham House Group and Non-Jurors, held views that were certainly not Cranmer's, though felt able to use the Book of Common Prayer without regarding it as at variance with their own beliefs.[20]

Dix's paucity of knowledge here meant that his remarks tended to be political and polemical rather than scholarly. Dix's views on the Cranmerian liturgy may be contrasted with that of A. H. Couratin: "If the history of the Common Prayer book evoked no immediate sympathy, it was not the

---

18. Old, *Patristic Roots of Reformed Worship.*

19. The most recent study is G. Jeannes, *Signs of God's Promise.*

20. Spinks, *Sacraments, Ceremonies and the Stuart Divines.*

less necessary to disseminate an accurate account of its nature."[21] Couratin was no lover of the Prayer Book's Communion rite, but appreciated Cranmer's workmanship and felt that if one held the same theological principles, it was a masterpiece. Dix's discussion took place in the penultimate chapter in *The Shape*, and there he suggested a way forward to experiment with a newer form, which was more in accordance with the "classical" shape than the 1662 Communion rite. However, he never addressed the question of a reform of the very rite that was in use at Nashdom, namely the then contemporary Roman rite, which by his own patristic standards, was equally in need of reform.

4. In Retrospect.

None of us comes to the past with entirely objective eyes. We usually select subjects and materials that are of interest to us now, and possibly of interest to our own contemporaries. We select and discard according to our beliefs and likes. Dix was no different. He had a profound unease with the Reformation and the Church of England liturgy, much preferring to seek an Anglican reunion with Rome and using the Roman rite. He thus selected and interpreted the liturgical past with an eye to affirming his own liturgical preferences, and discrediting a liturgy for which he had little sympathy. However, his method of doing this was to convict the Anglican liturgies of being the end of medieval degeneration, which could be rectified by appeal to patristic forms. This does not invalidate many of the points he made about the Anglican rite. His penultimate chapter in *The Shape* rightly suggested that in the context of the whole of liturgical history, the Book of Common Prayer is but a minor piece and of little interest to most non-Anglicans. However, patristic fundamentalism is not superior to Reformation fundamentalism.[22] Part of the integrity of serious liturgical scholarship is the need to assess a liturgy on its own grounds and in its own context, even if it is one that elicits little theological sympathy from the enquirer. Where Dix was right was that in 1945 he urged that the Church of England needed to move beyond the inertia that had set in after the defeat of the 1928 Book of Common Prayer, and strive to formulate contemporary forms beyond

21. Melrose, "Arthur Hubert Couratin. A Biographical Note," 12–13.

22. For an example of the latter, see Scales, *What Mean ye by this Service*, which argued that since Series 2 experimental Church of England service allowed the Agnus Dei, it taught transubstantiation and was a sell out to Rome.

Cranmer. The founding of a Liturgical Commission and the subsequent revisions that led to the Alternative Service Book, 1980, and then Common Worship, 2000, have been a response more than Dix could have imagined. But one wonders whether, like some contemporary Anglo-Papalists, he would have ignored the results, and simply used the post-Vatican II forms.

Published Academic Writings of Peter Toon[1]

Peter Toon's first piece appeared in the *Baptist Quarterly* (a publication of the Baptist Union of Great Britain) on the topic of "The Strict and Particular Baptists" in 1964 when he was studying for his bachelor of divinity at King's College, University of London. (*Strict* refers to admittance to Communion and *Particular* refers to the extent of the atonement.) His first book continued the theme of Calvinism and appeared in 1967 as *The Emergence of Hyper-Calvinism in English Nonconformity, 1689–1765*. It has a preface by Dr. J. I. Packer, and it was the cause of various invitations to the author to lecture in the United States.

This list does not include hundreds of articles and essays placed on the Internet between the late 1990s and 2009.

English Puritanism

The Emergence of Hyper-Calvinism (1967)
The Correspondence of John Owen (1970)
Puritans the Millennium (1970)
Puritans and Calvinism (1971)
God's Statesman (1972)
The University Orations of Dr. John Owen (1973)

Semipopular Doctrinal Writings

El Dios Siempre Presente

1. Previously published in Toon, *A Foretaste of Heaven*.

The Right of Private Judgment (1975)
Jesus Christ Is Lord (1978)
Free to Obey (1979)
God Here and Now (1979, also in Spanish)
God's Church for Today (1980)
God's Kingdom for Today (1980)
God's Salvation for Today (1980)
Protestant and Catholic (1983)
What's the Difference? (1983)
What We Believe (1984)
Your Conscience as Your Guide (1984)
General Godliness and True Piety (2000)

Serious Doctrinal Writing

Justification and Sanctification (1983)
The Ascension of Our Lord (1984)
Heaven and Hell (1986)
The End of Liberal Theology (1995)
Yesterday, Today and Forever (1996)
Our Triune God (1996, 2002)

Spirituality

About Turn: The Decisional Event of Conversion (1987)
Born Again (1987)
What Is Spirituality? (1989)
Spiritual Companions (1990, also in Korean)

Meditation

From Mind to Heart (1987)
Longing for Heaven (1987)
Meditating as a Christian (1991)
The Art of Meditating on Scripture (1993)
Meditating upon God's Word (1998)

Anglican Theology and Liturgy

The Ordinal and Its Revision (1974)
The Development of Doctrine in the Church (1979)
Evangelical Theology, 1833–1856 (1979)
The Anglican Way, Evangelical and Catholic (1983)
Britain's True Greatness (1984)
Let Women Be Women (1990)
Knowing God through the Liturgy (1992)
Proclaiming the Gospel through the Liturgy (1993)
Which Rite is Right? (1994)
Common Worship Considered (2003)
Reforming Forwards? (2003)
The Order for Holy Communion, 1662 (Annotated, 2004)
The Order for Holy Communion, 1928 (Annotated, 2004)
Same-Sex Affection, Holiness and Ordination (2005)
Worship without Dumbing Down (2005)
The Anglican Formularies and Holy Scripture (2006)
Anglican Identity (2006)
Episcopal Innovations 1960–2004 in ECUSA (2006)
The Order for Evening Prayer, 1662 (Annotated, 2007)
Mystical Washing and Spiritual Regeneration (2007)
On Salvation and the Church of Rome—Richard Hooker (2007)

Writings in Cooperation with Louis Tarsitano, Edited by Peter Toon

The Way, The Truth and the Life: The Anglican Walk (1998)
Dear Primates (2000)
Neither Archaic nor Obsolete (2003)
Neither Orthodoxy nor a Formulary (2004)

Books Edited by Peter Toon, Wholly or Partly

Puritans, the Millennium and the Future of Israel (1970)
John Charles Ryle, Evangelical Bishop (1976)
One God in Trinity (1980)
Real Questions (with David Field, 1982)
Let God Be God (1990)
A Guidebook to the Spiritual Life (1998)

Individual Essays in Books Edited by Others

"Anglicanism in Popish Dress," in *Tradition Renewed* (1986)
"Appreciating Mary Today," in *Chosen by God, Mary* (1989)
"The Articles and Homilies," in *The Study of Anglicanism* (1998)
"The Eames Commission and the Doctrine of Reception," in *To Mend the Net* (2001)
"The Formularies and the Limits of Diversity," in *To Mend the Net* (2001)
"Episcopalianism," in *Who Runs the Church?* (2004)
"Justification by Faith Alone," in *Justification and Sanctification* (2008)

Edited Dictionaries

The Compact Bible Dictionary (1987)
New International Version Bible Guide (1987)
The Concise Dictionary of the Christian Tradition (1989)
The Concise Evangelical Dictionary of Theology (1992)

Edited Prayer Books

Worshipping the Lord in the Anglican Way (2004)
An Anglican Prayer Book (2008), based on *The Book of Common Prayer* (1662, 1928, 1965)

Edited Classic Short Works on the Devotional Life

Introduction to the Devout Life, Saint Francis de Sales (1988)
Christ for All Seasons, Thomas à Kempis (1989)
Prayers for Families, Benjamin Jenks (1990)

Edited Magazines

Home Words, parish magazine insert for the Church of England, 1985–1990
Mandate, Prayer Book Society, USA, 1995–2008

Bibliography

Ackroyd, Peter. "He Followed the King's Devices and Desires." Review of *Thomas Cranmer* by Diarmaid MacCulloch. *The Times*, May 23, 1996, 38.

Armitage, F. *A History of the Collects.* London: Weare, 1919.

Atkinson, Nigel. *Richard Hooker and the Authority of Scripture, Tradition, and Reason.* Carlisle, UK: Paternoster, 1997.

Ayris, Paul, and David Selwyn. *Thomas Cranmer: Churchman and Scholar.* Woodbridge, UK: Boydell, 1993.

Bailey, Simon. *A Tactful God: Gregory Dix Priest, Monk and Scholar.* Leominster, UK: Gracewing, 1995.

Beckwith, Roger T. "Lay Celebration of Communion." *Latimer Comment 49*, 1–5. Oxford: Latimer House, n.d.

Bell, Duncan S. A. "The Cambridge School and World Politics: Critical Theory, History and Conceptual Change." No pages. Online: http://www.theglobalsite.ac.uk/press/103bell.htm

Berger, Peter. *The Heretical Imperative: Contemporary Possibilities of Religious Affirmation.* Garden City, NY: Anchor, 1979.

Bernard. G. W. *The King's Reformation: Henry VIII and the Remaking of the English Church.* New Haven, CT: Yale University Press, 2005.

Bicknell, E. J. *A Theological Introduction to the Thirty-Nine Articles of the Church of England.* 1919. Reprint. London: Longmans, 1955.

Bloom, H. *Jesus and Yahweh: The Names Divine.* New York: Riverhead, 2005.

Booty, John. *The Book of Common Prayer 1559: The Elizabethan Prayer Book.* The Folger Shakespeare Library. Charlottesville, VA: University Press of Virginia, 1976.

———. "The Quest for the Historical Hooker." *The Churchman* 80.3 (1966) 185–93.

Bradshaw, Paul F., M. E. Johnson, L .E. Phillips, and H. W. Attridge. *The Apostolic Tradition: A Commentary.* Minneapolis, MN: Fortress, 2002.

Bradshaw, Paul. "Gregory Dix." In *They Shaped Our Worship: Essays on Anglican Liturgists,* edited by Christopher Irvine, 111–16. London: SPCK, 1998.

Brent, Allen. *Hippolytus and the Roman Church in the Third Century: Communities in Tension before the Emergence of a Monarch Bishop.* Leiden: Brill, 1995.

Brightman, F. E. *The English Rite: Being a Synopsis of the Sources and Revisions of the Book of Common Prayer with an Introduction and Appendix.* 2 vols. London: Rivingtons, 1915.

Bromiley, G. W. *Thomas Cranmer: Archbishop and Martyr.* London: Church Book Room, 1956.

Brooks, Peter Newman. *Cranmer in Context.* Cambridge: Lutterworth, 1989.

Brown, S. L." Joel." In *A New Commentary on Holy Scripture: Including the Apocrypha*, edited by C. Gore. 1928. Reprint. London: SPCK, 1943.

Buchanan, Colin. *The End of the Offertory: An Anglican Study*. Cambridge, UK: Grove, 1978.

Calvin, John. *Institutes of the Christian Religion*. Translated by H. Beveridge. 2 vols. London: Clarke, 1962.

Cranmer, Thomas. *Miscellaneous Writings and Letters of Thomas Cranmer*. Edited for the Parker Society by John Edmund Cox. Cambridge: Cambridge University Press, 1846.

————. *The Works of Thomas Cranmer*. Vol. 2. Edited for the Parker Society by John Edmund Cox. Cambridge: Cambridge University Press, 1846.

————. *The Works of Thomas Cranmer*. Edited by G. E. Duffield. Berkshire, UK: Sutton Courtenay, 1965.

————. *Writings of the Rev. Dr. Thomas Cranmer, Archbishop of Canterbury and Martyr, 1556*. Philadelphia: Presbyterian Board of Publication, 1842.

Cuming, G. J. *The Godly Order: Text and Studies Relating to the Book of Common Prayer*. London: Alcuin Club, 1983.

————. *A History of Anglican Liturgy*. 2nd ed. London: Macmillan, 1982.

Davie, M. *The Diaries of Evelyn Waugh*. London: Weidenfeld and Nicolson, 1976.

Dix, Gregory. *The Shape of the Liturgy*. London: Dacre, 1945.

————. *The Theology of Confirmation in Relation to Baptism*. Westminster, UK: Dacre, 1946.

————. *The Treatise on the Apostolic Tradition of St. Hippolytus of Rome*. London: SPCK, 1937.

Dudley, M. R. *The Collect in Anglican Liturgy: Texts and Sources 1549–1989*. Collegeville, MN: Liturgical, 1994.

Dunlop, Colin. *Thomas Cranmer: Two Studies*. London: SPCK, 1956.

Dunn, John. "The History of Political Theory." In *The History of Political Theory and Other Essays*, 11–38. Cambridge: Cambridge University Press, 1996.

Edwards, D. "Faith with Thanksgiving: Quincentenary Tribute to Thomas Cranmer." *Church Times*, June 39, 1989, 11.

Farley, Benjamin Wirt. *Treatises against the Anabaptists and against the Libertines*. Grand Rapids: Baker, 1982.

Felce, B. G. "Toplady's View of Doctrinal Continuity after the Reformation." In *The Evangelical Succession in the Church of England*, edited by David N. Samuel, 30–39. Cambridge: Clarke, 1979.

The First and Second Prayer Books of Edward VI. London: Everyman's Library, 1968.

Fisher, J. D. C. *Confirmation Then and Now*. London: SPCK, 1978.

Gadamer, H.-G. *Truth and Method*. Translated by J. A. Weinsheimer. Rev. ed. New York: Continuum, 2006.

Hankey, Wayne, J. "The Thirty-Nine Articles as a Theological System." In *The Thirty-Nine Articles*, edited by G. Richmond Bridge, 1–11. Charlottetown, PE: St Peter's, 1990.

Hatchett, M. J. "Prayer Books." In *The Study of Anglicanism*, edited by S. Sykes et al., 131–43. London: SPCK, 1988.

Heinze, Rudolph W. *The Proclamations of the Tudor Kings*. Cambridge: Cambridge University Press, 1976.

Hippolytus. *On the Apostolic Tradition*. Edited by Alistair Steward-Sykes and John Behr. Crestwood, NY: St. Vladimir's Press, 2001.

Hogan, Michael. *The Sectarian Strand: Religion in Australian History.* Ringwood, Australia: Penguin, 1987.

The Homilies. Bishopstone, UK: Brynmill, 2006.

Hooker, Richard. *Hooker's Ecclesiastical Polity Book VIII.* Introduction by R. A. Houk. New York: Columbia University Press, 1931.

———. *Of the Laws of Ecclesiastical Polity.* In *The Works of Richard Hooker,* 6 vols., edited by W. Speed Hill. The Folger Library Edition. Cambridge: Harvard University Press, 1977.

Hughes, Phillip E. *The Theology of the English Reformers.* 1980. Reprint. Eugene, OR: Wipf and Stock, 2009.

Jeannes, G. *Signs of God's Promise: Thomas Cranmer's Sacramental Theology and the Book of Common Prayer.* London: T. & T. Clark, 2008.

Jones, Simon. *The Sacramental Life: Gregory Dix and His Writings.* Norwich, UK: Canterbury, 2007.

Kirby, W. J. Torrance. *Richard Hooker's Doctrine of the Royal Supremacy.* Leiden: Brill, 1990.

Knox, E. A. *The Tractarian Movement, 1833–1845.* London: Putnam, 1933.

Lyon, R. P. *The Sign of Jonah.* Canada: Graphikos, 2005.

MacCulloch, Diarmaid. *Thomas Cranmer.* New Haven, CT: Yale University Press, 1996.

MacIntyre, Alasdair. *After Virtue.* 2nd ed. Notre Dame, IN: University of Notre Dame Press, 1984.

———. *Whose Justice? Which Rationality?* Notre Dame, IN: University of Notre Dame Press, 1988.

Manschreck, C. L. *Melanchthon on Christian Doctrine: Loci Communes 1555.* New York: Oxford University Press, 1965.

Merle D'Aubinge, Jean Henri. *Vindication of Cranmer's Character from the Attacks of Mr. Macaulay: A Letter to the Most Noble the Marquis of Cholmodeley.* London Nisbet, 1849.

Melrose, Michael. "Arthur Hubert Couratin. A Biographical Note." In *The Sacrifice of Praise: Studies and Themes of Thanksgiving and Redemption in the Central Prayers of the Eucharist and Baptismal Liturgies,* edited Bryan D. Spinks, 11–12. Rome: CLV, 1981.

Michell, G. A. *Landmarks in Liturgy.* London: DLT, 1961.

Neill, Stephen. *Anglicanism.* London: Mowbray, 1977.

Nichols, John, ed. *Narratives of the Days of the Reformation.* London: Camden Society, 1859.

Null, Ashley. "Thomas Cranmer and the Lively Word." *Anglican Way* 35.1 (2012) 7–9.

———. *Thomas Cranmer's Doctrine of Repentance: Renewing the Power of Love.* Oxford: Oxford University Press, 2000.

O'Donovan, Joan Lockwood. "The Church's Worship and the Moral Life: An Anglican Contribution to Trinitarian Ethic." In *Creed and Conscience: Essays in Honour of A. James Reimer,* edited by Jeremy M. Bergen et al., 181–96. Kitchener, ON: Pandora, 2007.

———. "A Reformation Ethics: Proclamation and Jurisdiction as Determinants of Moral Agency and Action." *Philosophia Reformata* 71.1 (2006) 58–78.

O'Donovan, Oliver, and J. Lockwood O'Donovan. *From Irenaeus to Grotius: A Sourcebook in Christian Political Thought.* Grand Rapids: Eerdmans, 1999.

Old, H. O. *The Patristic Roots of Reformed Worship.* Zürich: Theologischer, 1970.

Packer, J. I., and Roger Beckwith. *The Thirty-Nine Articles: Their Place and Use Today.* Latimer Studies 20–21. 1984. Reprint. Vancouver, BC: Regent College, 2007.

Parris, Matthew. "A Funeral Teaches Me that Gray was Wrong in His Elegy about the Loneliness of Virtue." *The Spectator* 5 May, 2009. Online:http://www.spectator.co.uk/columnists/all/3592136/another-voice.thtml

Ridley, Jaspar. *Thomas Cranmer.* Oxford: Oxford University Press, 1962.

Rivers, Julian. *The Law of Organized Religions: Between Establishment and Secularism.* Oxford: Oxford University Press, 2010.

Rogers, Thomas. *The Catholic Doctrine of the Church of England: An Exposition of the Thirty-Nine Articles.* Cambridge: Cambridge University Press, 1854.

Scales, Derek. *What Mean Ye by This Service.* Dereham, UK: Truth and Faith Committee, 1969.

Sisson, C. J. *The Judicious Marriage of Mr Hooker.* Cambridge: Cambridge University Press, 1940.

Spinks, Bryan D. "Cranmer, Baptism and Christian Nurture, or, Toronto Revisited." *Studia Liturgica* 32.1 (2002) 98–110.

———. "Mis-Shapen: Gregory Dix and the Four Action Shape of the Liturgy." *Lutheran Quarterly* 4 (1990) 161–77.

———. *Sacraments, Ceremonies and the Stuart Divines: Sacramental Theology and Liturgy in England and Scotland 1603–1662.* Aldershot, UK: Ashgate, 2002.

———. *Two Faces of Elizabethan Anglican Theology: Sacraments and Salvation in the Thought of William Perkins and Richard Hooker.* Lanham, NY: Scarecrow, 1999.

Stephenson, Kenneth. W. *Gregory Dix—Twenty Five Years On.* Grove Liturgical Study 10. Cambridge, UK: Grove, 1977.

Talmon, S. "The Crystallisation of the 'Canon of Hebrew Scriptures' in Light of the Biblical Scrolls from Qumran." In *The Bible as Book: The Hebrew Bible and the Judaean Desert Discoveries*, edited by E .D. Herbert and Emanuel Tov, 5–20. New Castle, DE: Oak Knoll, 2002.

Taylor, Charles. *A Secular Age.* Cambridge, MA: Harvard University Press, 2007.

———. *Sources of the Self: The Making of the Modern Identity.* Cambridge: Cambridge University Press, 1992.

Toon, Peter. *The Anglican Way: Evangelical and Catholic.* 1983. Reprint. Eugene, OR: Wipf and Stock, 2010.

———. *The Development of Doctrine in the Church.* Grand Rapids: Eerdmans: 1979.

———. *The End of Liberal Theology: Contemporary Challenges to Evangelical Orthodoxy.* Wheaton, IL: Crossway, 1995.

———. *A Foretaste of Heaven amidst Suffering.* Reprint. Eugene, OR: Wipf and Stock, 2010.

Townsend, G., and S. R. Cattley. *The Acts and Monuments of John Foxe,* vol. 8. New York: AMS, 1965.

Upton, W. Prescott. *The Churchman's History of the Oxford Movement.* London: Church Book Room, 1933.

Wannenwetsch, Bernd. *Political Worship: Ethics for Christian Citizens.* Translated by M. Kohl. Oxford: Oxford University Press, 2004.

Weston, A. *Apologia pro Fide Mea.* Unpublished manuscript.

Whitgift, J. *The Defence of the Answer to the Admonition against the Reply of T. C.* [Thomas Cartwright]. Tract 13. In *The Works of John Whitgift*, vol. 3, edited by J. Ayre for The Parker Society, 39–40. Cambridge: Cambridge University Press, 1853.

Williams, Rowan. "The Archbishop of Canterbury's Sermon," *Mandate*, May/June 2006. Online:http://www.pbsusa.org.

———. *The Word of God in the Anglican Tradition.* No pages. Online: http://www.archbishopofcanterbury.org/articles.php/2282/the-word-of-god-in-anglican-tradition-archbishop-addresses-focolare-bishops.

Index

Index